Death Masks

Faces for Eternity

Death Masks

Faces for Eternity

© Copyright 2023
All Rights Reserved

ISBN - 9798398010909

Credits

Written and Independently Published:
Ron Celano

Cover Artwork

Ron Celano

Disclaimer

While the author has made every effort to provide accurate Internet addresses and other contact information at the time of this publication, neither the publisher nor the author assumes any responsibility for errors or for changes that occur before or after publication. Furthermore, the publisher does not have any control over and does not assume any responsibility for third party web sites or their content.

Copyright Notice

Copyright law protects this publication. To photocopy or distribute pirated copies or provide links to pirated copies or reproduce by any method without the approval of the author is an infringement of the copyright law. Anyone who reproduces or provides links to copyrighted matter is subject to substantial penalties and assessments for each infringement.

Images

Images were obtained from the public domain, CC-BY license, from royalty free sources or granted permission to use by the source or author. All images are captioned with a link to the corresponding website. Additionally, the writer makes no guarantee that the image for any item is authentic. Nevertheless, it is assumed to be a typical representation of said items.

Table of Contents

Preface 1

Introduction 3

The History of Death Masks 5
    Ancient Egypt 5
    Ancient Greece and Rome 7
    Other Ancient Cultures 8
    Renaissance and Early Modern Era 9
    An Ongoing Tradition 11
    The Future of Death Masks 11

The Science of Death Masks 14
    The process of making a death mask 14
    Death Masks as Forensic Evidence 15
    Death Masks and the Study of Physiognomy .. 17

The Influence of Death Masks on Art and Literature 19
    The Role of Death Masks in Art 19
    The Role of Death Masks in Literature 21

The Masters Behind the Masks 23
        Jean-Antoine Houdon 23
        Madame Tussaud 24
        James De Ville 24
        Thomas Woolner 25

Carlo Bartolomeo Rastrelli 25
  Franz Xaver Messerschmidt 26
  Count Joseph Deym von Stritetz 26
  Domenico Brucciani 27
  Nick Reynolds 27
Famous Death Masks 29
  Royalty & Nobility 29
    King Henry IV of France 29
    Marie Louise Gonzaga 30
    Queen Elizabeth I of England 32
    King Charles XII of Sweden 34
    Alexander I of Russia 35
    Mary Queen of Scots 37
    Frederick the Great 39
    Louise of Prussia 41
    King Henry VII of England 42
  Military Leaders 44
    Henry Warner Slocum 44
    G. R. Mirabeau 46
    Oliver Cromwell 48
    Admiral George Dewey 50
    Jozef Pilsudski 52
    Michael Collins 54
    Ulysses S. Grant 56
    Robert E. Lee 57

Pancho Villas 59
William Tecumseh Sherman 61
François Athanase Charette 63

Philosophers 65
Immanuel Kant 65
Friedrich Nietzsche 66
Giacomo Leopardi 68
Jeremy Bentham 70
Edmund Burke 72

Poets, Novelists, & Writers 74
James Joyce 74
Walt Whitman 76
Kornel Makuszyński 78
Goldwin Smith 79
Sir Walter Scott 81
Celia Thaxter 83
William Makepeace Thackery 84
Edward Kean 86
Torquato Tasso 87
Samual Johnson 89
Dante Alighieri 93
John Keats 94
Samuel Taylor Coleridge 96
Friedrich Schiller 97
Heinrich Heine 99

Victor Hugo 101
Carl Michael Bellman 103
Jonathan Swift 104
James Hogg 106

Scientists, Chemists, Physicists, & Doctors 107

Louis Agassiz 107
Arthor H. Compton 109
Sir Isaac Newton 111
Alfred Nobel 113
Joseph Leidy 115
Dr. John Hunter 117
Blaise Pascal 119

Composers 121

Ludwig van Beethoven 121
Felix Mendelssohn 123
Franz Schubert 125
Richard Wagner 126
Franz Liszt 128
Johann Strauss II 130
Pyotr Ilyich Tchaikovsky 131
Wolfgang Amadeus Mozart 133
Frederic Chopin 135
Josef Leopold Zvonar 136

Artists & Sculptors 138

Josef Moroder Lusenberg ... 138
Benjamin Robert Hayden ... 139
Sir Thomas Lawrence ... 141
J. M. W. Turner ... 142
Dante Gabriel Rossetti ... 144
Wilhelm von Kaulback ... 146
Antonio Canova ... 148
James John Audubon ... 150
Jacques-Louis David ... 152
Vojtech Preissig ... 154
Egon Schiele ... 155
Hiram Powers ... 157

Political Leaders & Activists ... 158
Napoleon Bonaparte ... 158
Robert Emmet ... 160
Joseph Stalin ... 162
Thomas Paine ... 163
Aaron Burr ... 165
Daniel O'Connell ... 167
William McKinley ... 169
Theodore Roosevelt ... 171
Vladimir Lenin ... 173
Lorenzo De' Medici ... 175
Eva Peron ... 176

Politicians & Statesmen ... 179

John Philpot Curran 179

Lord Palmerston...180

Benjamin Disraeli..182

Daniel Webster..184

Jean Paul Marat 186

Henry George 188

Count Cavour 189

Charles Sumner...191

Maximillian Robespierre..193

Religious Leaders, Theologians, & Notables
....195

Martin Luther 195

Martin Luther King Jr..197

St. Ignatius of Loyola..199

Jose Maria Morelos 200

Pope Pius IX 202

Thomas Chalmers 204

Harry Edwards 205

Joseph and Hyrum Smith 206

Criminals 208

Sacco and Vanzetti 208

Ned Kelly 210

Richard Parker 212

William Palmer 214

John Dillinger...216

James Bloomfield Rush 217
Burke and Hare 219
Heinrich Himmler 221
Actors 223
David Garrick 223
Edmund Kean.. 225
John Edward McCullough 227
Dion Boucicault 229
Lawrence Barrett 231
Edwin Booth.. 232
Others.. 234
Maria F. Malibran... 234
Alios Senefelder.. 235
Ben Caunt.. 237
L.C. La Bourdonnais 238
Max Reinhardt... 240
Marc Isambard Brunel Sr... 242
Richard Brinsley Sheridan 244
Dolly... 245
Collecting Death Masks 247
Conclusion... 251
Additional Resources 253
Image References 263

Preface

Masks have been used throughout history for a wide variety of purposes and have been made from a range of materials. They have been made from woods, metals, shells, fibers, ivory, clay, horn, stone, feathers, leather, furs, paper, cloth, and corn husks. Surface treatments have ranged from rugged simplicity to intricate carving and from gaudy adornments to polished woods and mosaics. Masks of the world display virtually infinite variety, from the simplest of crude "false faces" held by a handle to complete head coverings designed with ingenious movable parts.

Masks have been used for funerary purposes, as protection in warfare, during theater performances, and by impersonators of gods during religious ceremonies. The death mask of Egyptian pharaoh Tutankhamun is made of gold, precious stones, and glass inlay. The mask of Agamemnon, the king of Mycenae in Homer's Iliad, is also a famous ancient mask. In Japan, mask-wearing symbolized "modernity" during the Spanish flu epidemic. In China, mask-wearing has a long history, and a pneumonic plague epidemic in China in 1910-11 sparked widespread mask-wearing there.

The Native American masks of the northwest coast of America and Alaska are known for their transformational qualities. These masks use elements of the formline style, a term coined in 1965 to describe the characteristics of northwest coast visual culture. Later, brighter and more durable synthetic colors were introduced.

It seemed that writing a book about the different types and styles of masks throughout history would be an over whelming project for this author. Therefore, it was decided to write about the most fascinating masks of all - death masks [1]. Human and animal death masks have been created for centuries to preserve the memory of the deceased. This book is not only a tribute to the art of death masks but also a celebration of life and the memories that were left behind. The stories and experiences shared in this book offer a glimpse into the lives of some famous and not so famous people who have come before us, and inspire readers to cherish their own memories and the memories of their loved ones.

Please note that funeral masks, totenmaskes (buried with the dead) and death masks are used interchangeably throughout this book. In addition, the images herein may or may not be an original mask. Life masks may be mentioned briefly when discussing those that created both life and death masks.

Introduction

Death masks are usually of wax or plaster casts made from a mold formed from the face of a dead individual [2]. They are true portraits, although changes are occasionally made to the eyes of the mask to make it appear as though the subject were alive. From the time of ancient Egypt they have served as aids to portrait sculptors, and for the last few centuries they have been kept as mementos of the dead.

Death masks have been used for various purposes throughout history. They were used in the making of effigies, so that dead royalty could travel their land and people could pay their final respects to an imperishable leader, no matter how long the trip. They were also used as a way to preserve an image of a person, whether they were famous or not. Death masks have been used by scientists to record variations in human physiognomy. Anthropologists used such masks to study physiognomic features in famous people.

They have been made of famous people throughout history, including Benjamin Franklin, Ludwig van Beethoven, and Napoleon. Others have been made of royalty, such as the death mask of Henry VII and Queen Elizabeth I of England. Death masks have been used to capture a moment that's often hidden away from plain sight. They offer a real-life glimpse into the moment shortly after death, something few people experience.

In this book about death masks, readers will learn about the history, legends, myths, and interesting facts surrounding this unique art form. The book will explore the different uses of death masks throughout history, from effigies to mementos of the dead. It will also delve into the science behind death masks and how they have been used to study physiognomic features of people. The book will feature death masks of notable people, and the stories of their lives. Readers will gain a new appreciation for this unique art form and its place in human history.

The History of Death Masks

Ancient Egypt:

Death masks have been an integral part of ancient Egyptian culture for thousands of years [3]. These masks were created as a way to preserve the appearance of the deceased and were believed to help the individual in the afterlife. They were thought to help the individual navigate through the dangers and challenges of the afterlife and to ensure that they were properly recognized and honored by the gods.

The practice of creating death masks in ancient Egypt began during the Old Kingdom period, which lasted from around 2575 BC to 2150 BC. During this time, death masks were primarily reserved for pharaohs and other members of the royal family. These masks were often made from precious materials such as gold, silver, or bronze, and were adorned with intricate designs and symbols.

During the Middle Kingdom period, which lasted from around 2055 BC to 1650 BC, death masks became more common among non-royal members of society. However, these masks were typically made of less expensive materials such as plaster or cartonnage, which is a type of papier-mâché made from linen and plaster.

The New Kingdom period, which lasted from around 1550 BC to 1070 BC, is often referred to as the "golden age" of death masks in ancient

Egypt. During this time, death masks became more widely used and were often made for other members of society as well.

Fig 1

One of the most famous examples of an ancient Egyptian death mask is that of King Tutankhamun. His golden death mask was discovered in 1922 by Howard Carter and remains one of the most iconic images of ancient Egypt. The mask, which covers the head and shoulders of the mummy, is made from solid gold and is highly detailed, featuring the pharaoh's facial features and a cobra and vulture representing the protective goddesses of Upper and Lower Egypt.

In addition to their religious significance, death masks also had practical purposes. They were used to identify the deceased and to ensure that their bodies were properly prepared for burial. The masks were also used as a way to create a visual record of the individual's appearance and to commemorate their life and achievements.

Death masks played a significant role in ancient Egyptian culture and continue to fascinate people today with their intricate designs and haunting beauty. They offer a glimpse into the beliefs and customs of one of the world's greatest ancient civilizations and continue to be an important part of our understanding of history and art.

Ancient Greece and Rome:

Death masks were a significant part of ancient Greek and Roman funerary practices. The process of making a death mask involved taking a cast or impression of the deceased person's face after death. The masks were usually made from wax, plaster, or gold, and they served as a likeness of the deceased for burial or commemorative purposes.

In ancient Greece, the practice of making death masks was most prevalent during the Mycenaean period. The Mycenaean civilization produced a series of golden funerary masks, known as the death masks of Mycenae. These were originally discovered in a burial site called Grave Circle A in the ancient Greek city of Mycenae. These masks were found on the buried bodies of six adult males and one male child, and they were adorned with intricate designs and gold leaf. Interestingly, there were no women who had masks.

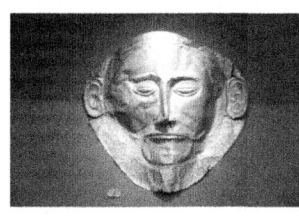
Fig 2

One of the most famous masks is the Mask of Agamemnon, which is made of gold and was discovered in Mycenae in 1876 by the German archaeologist

Heinrich Schliemann. Despite its name, it is unclear whether the mask actually depicts Agamemnon or another individual.

In ancient Rome, death masks were also used to commemorate deceased individuals. However, their use was more widespread, and they were not restricted to only the upper classes. The Romans made death masks from wax (called "imagines"), which were molded onto the face of the deceased person. These masks were often painted to give a more lifelike appearance. The masks were then displayed at funerals, and they were also used as a way to remember the dead.

The reasons for making death masks in ancient Greece and Rome were varied. In Greece, it was believed that the masks served as a way to ensure that the deceased person's spirit would recognize their body and return to it after death. It was also believed that the masks had a protective function and could ward off evil spirits.

Other Ancient Cultures:

Apart from Egypt, Greece, and Rome, there are other cultures that used death masks as well. For instance, in the pre-Columbian era, the Moche civilization of Peru created death masks of their rulers and other important people. These masks were made of copper and gold and were often buried with the deceased.

In Japan, death masks were known as "kagemi" were used to preserve the memory of the deceased. These masks were made of wax or paper and were often painted to resemble the person's face.

In Mexico, death masks were used during the Day of the Dead festival. These masks were made of sugar or chocolate and were decorated with colorful icing.

In Africa, death masks were used by the Yoruba people of Nigeria. These masks were made of wood and were used in funerary rites to honor the deceased.

Renaissance and Early Modern Era:

Death masks were a popular art form during the Renaissance and Early Modern eras, which lasted roughly from the 14th century to the 18th century. They were primarily used as a way to preserve the likeness of the deceased for future generations to remember them by, and they were often displayed in public or private settings as a means of honoring the deceased.

During the Renaissance, death masks became a popular way for artists to study and perfect their craft. Many artists used death masks as a model for creating realistic sculptures or paintings of the deceased, and some even incorporated the masks into their art. Death masks also had cultural significance during this time period. They were often commissioned by royalty, nobility, or other important figures as a way of immortalizing their legacy. The masks were seen as a way to capture the essence of the person's character and to preserve their memory for generations to come. Death masks were also used as a way to honor martyrs and other religious figures, and they were often displayed in churches or other religious settings.

In the Early Modern era, death masks continued to be used for similar purposes, but they also became more widely available to the general public. People could purchase or commission death masks of their loved ones as a way to remember them after death. These masks were often displayed in the home and passed down as family heirlooms.

Today, death masks are still culturally important, although they are less common than they were during the Renaissance and Early Modern eras. Many museums and art galleries have collections of death masks, and they are often used as a way to study the history and culture of a particular time period or individual. Death masks are also seen as a way to connect with the past and to remember those who have come before us. They serve as a reminder of our mortality and the fleeting nature of life, and they encourage us to appreciate the time we have and to live our lives to the fullest.

An Ongoing Tradition:

While death masks are not as common today, some are still being made for well-known celebrities and everyday people. Artists are reclaiming this practice as more people reconsider modern practices around grief and loss.

In the 21st century modern technology and artistic techniques offer new and unique ways to capture the likeness of the deceased providing insight into what happens to our bodies and our legacies when we die [4].

A group of design buffs at MIT, as part of the "Mediated Matter Research Cluster," is using high definition 3D printing software and 3D images of vital DNA to create intricate and detailed death masks. The masks can be made in a variety of materials, including bronze, resin, or even chocolate.

The Future of Death Masks:

With advancements in technology and the changing attitudes towards death and memorialization, the future of death masks is uncertain. One possibility for the future of death masks is their continued use as a form of art. Death masks have been used by artists for centuries as a way to capture the unique features of their subjects. Some contemporary artists continue to create death masks, often using modern materials such as silicone and 3D printing technology to create highly detailed and accurate replicas. These masks can be used to create sculptures, paintings, and other works of art.

Another potential future for death masks is their use in the field of forensics. Death masks can provide valuable information about a person's facial structure, which can be used to help identify individuals in criminal investigations or missing person's cases. In some cases, forensic specialists have also used 3D printing technology to create replicas of death masks to aid in identification.

As attitudes towards death and memorialization continue to evolve, it is possible that death masks may become more personalized and accessible. With the rise of the "death positivity" movement, which seeks to normalize discussions and attitudes towards death, more people may begin to embrace the idea of having someone create their own death masks as a way to leave a lasting legacy [5]. Advances in technology may make it easier for individuals to create their own death masks at home, using materials such as alginate or silicone.

Overall, the future of death masks is uncertain, but it is clear that they will continue to hold a significant place in the realms of art, history, and forensic science. Whether they continue to be used primarily for historical preservation and artistic expression or become more personalized and accessible to the general public, death masks will continue to be a fascinating and poignant symbol of mortality and remembrance.

In conclusion, death masks have been used in various cultures for centuries to honor the deceased and establish a connection with the spirit world. They were also used to protect the dead from malevolent spirits. While some cultures used stylized versions of human faces, others created impressions of specific individuals. Death masks have served an important purpose in preserving the memory of those who have passed away and telling their stories. Although the use of death masks has declined with the invention of photography, they remain an important part of art, culture, and history. The practice of grieving and mourning varies across cultures, and death masks are just one example of the diverse ways in which different cultures honor and remember their dead.

The Science of Death Masks

The process of making a death mask:

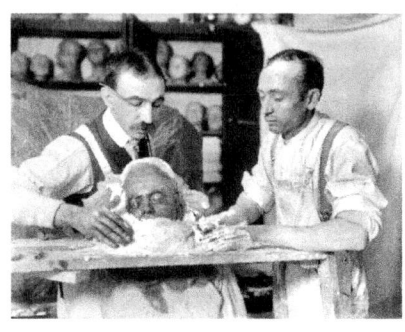

Fig 3

Historically, a death mask was a plaster or wax cast of a mold that is taken from the face of a deceased person. While not only a medical practice done by physicians, artists or sculptors also made plaster casts of the recently deceased.

To create a death mask, a mold must be taken from the face of the deceased as soon as possible after death, typically within the first few hours, before bloating and the elements distort the character and expression on the face. The face and head are oiled or greased, and then plaster bandages are applied to create the mold. The bandages are layered on the face to capture the details. Several layers are applied to strengthen the mold.

A modern method is to use an alginate gel, the same material used by dentists to make impressions of teeth, as a molding compound [6]. To make a death mask using alginate gel, one should mix half a kilogram of alginate with one liter of water and pour it over the face of the deceased. The bandages are carefully placed over the gel, working them to the contours of the face.

Once the mold hardens it is removed and placed face down in a container of sand. A depression is made in the sand to accept the mold and used to support it during the casting process. Then the mold is filled with plaster or wax. After the cast material hardens the mold is removed from the sand and the cast is removed from the mold. At this point any imperfections can be corrected. Finally, the mask is finished, and can be used as a memento of the dead or as a model for future portraits or busts.

Death Masks as Forensic Evidence:

In addition to serving as sentimental relics, death masks also historically played an important role in forensics. Before the widespread availability and use of forensic photography, pathologists would use death masks to preserve the facial features of unidentified bodies, so that relatives of the deceased could recognize them if they were seeking a missing person. While death masks may not be as commonly used in modern forensics as they once were, they can still be a valuable tool for investigators looking to identify an individual or to gather evidence [7].

One of the primary uses of death masks in forensics is in identifying the remains of individuals whose identity is unknown. By comparing the facial features captured in a death mask to images of missing persons or other potential matches, investigators may be able to make a positive identification. Additionally, death masks can be used to gather evidence in cases where the cause of death is unclear or there is suspicion of foul play. For example, if a death mask reveals injuries or trauma to the face that were not initially observed by investigators, this could lead to a re-examination of the death scene and potentially uncover new evidence.

Despite the potential benefits of using death masks in forensics, there are also some drawbacks and limitations to their use. For one, not all deaths are amenable to the creation of a death mask. In cases where the face has been severely disfigured or mutilated, it may be impossible to create a usable mask. Additionally, death masks are not always accurate representations of the individual's appearance in life, as the process of death can cause changes to the face and skin that may distort the features. As such, it is important that investigators take these limitations into account when using death masks as evidence in a forensic investigation.

Death Masks and the Study of Physiognomy:

The study of physiognomy has a long history, with its roots in antiquity [8]. It is a pseudoscientific practice that aims to discern an individual's personality, character, or even fate based on their physical features. In the 18th and 19th centuries, death masks were used to permanently record the features of unknown corpses for purposes of identification in Europe and the United States. Some notable figures in history, including Leonardo da Vinci and Johann Wolfgang von Goethe, had an interest in physiognomy, although it is not clear if either of them actually practiced it. Death masks have also been used in ethnography, archaeology, criminology, and race studies as well.

In the study of death masks through physiognomy, researchers aim to discern the personality and character traits of the deceased based on their physical features. For example, some researchers have claimed that the death mask of Napoleon Bonaparte shows a prominent brow and a hooked nose, which are seen as indicative of ambition and an aggressive personality. However, it is important to note that these claims are highly speculative and lack scientific basis. Death masks were also used to study the physiognomic features of famous people and notorious criminals. One example of a famous person whose death mask has been studied is Beethoven.

Despite the lack of scientific evidence supporting the practice of physiognomy, it continues to be studied by some researchers today. In recent years, there has been renewed interest in the study of physiognomy, with some researchers claiming that facial features can provide insight into a person's mental health or criminal tendencies. However, these claims have been met with criticism and skepticism from the scientific community, as there is little empirical evidence to support them.

The Influence of Death Masks on Art and Literature

The Role of Death Masks in Art:

Death masks have had a significant influence in art throughout history [9]. They have been used for various purposes, including the making of effigies so that dead royalty could travel their land and people could pay their final respects to an imperishable leader. Death masks were also used as a reference tool before the invention of photography, for use in the making of portraits.

One purpose of the death mask from the Middle-Ages until the 19th century was to serve as a model for sculptors in creating statues and busts of a deceased person. They were often used to preserve the likeness of the dead family member and were displayed at public funerals.

The use of death masks in art often blurred the lines between mourning and remembrance. They have been the subject of many artistic creations, from paintings and sculptures to photographs and mixed media. For example, the visual artist Max Siedentopf produced a series of tongue-in-cheek photographs inspired by homemade face masks, in his controversial series *How to Survive a Deadly*, exploring how masks have appeared in art.

Soviet artist Merkurov elevated the death mask from a simple mold to an art form. After casting the subject's head, he often transformed the work into a full sculpture, adding hair and clothing. His best-known work is his monumental death mask-turned-statue of Leo Tolstoy, which shows the writer in a kind of physical limbo between life and death.

Death masks have also been used in contemporary art. British artist Nick Reynolds runs a business called "Memorial Casts" making death (and life) masks. He believes that he's the only specialist of his kind in Britain, working out of a modest flat in Archway, in north London.

Fig 4

One of the most famous works of art featuring death masks is the "Masks Confronting Death" (1888) by James Ensor. The painting depicts a group of masks staring at and mocking the central figure of death, highlighting the power of death and the inevitability of mortality.

In conclusion, death masks have been an important cultural and artistic element for thousands of years, preserving the image of the deceased as well as inspiring artistic creations that explore the themes of death, mourning, and remembrance.

The Role of Death Masks in Literature:

Death masks have been a popular topic in literature, representing not only the physical likeness of the deceased but also the emotional and symbolic implications of death. According to a study published in *Advances in Psychiatric Treatment*, death and dying in literature are often explored through personal accounts, literature as a structure for thoughts, and as a literary device symbolizing societal decay.

In literature, the mask is used as a symbol to explore deeper meanings and interpretations. The use of masks in literature is explored in an essay titled *Importance of a Mask in Literature*, which describes how masks are used as a symbol in poetry, prose, and drama. In *The Masque of the Red Death*, a short story by Edgar Allan Poe, the use of the "Red Death" mask represents the end of life and the inevitable nature of death. The mask is a significant device used to create a specific atmosphere that emphasizes the theme of the story.

Jim Butcher's 2003 novel, *Death Masks*, is the fifth novel in *The Dresden Files*, his first published series that follows the character of Harry Dresden, professional wizard [10]. Charles

Dickens also used death masks in his writing to explore the theme of death and the fear of mortality.

In conclusion, death masks play a significant role in literature, representing the physical and emotional likeness of the deceased, societal expectations, and deeper meanings and interpretations. The use of masks in literature is explored in a variety of contexts, including personal accounts of death, preservation of memory, and as a symbol of identity and societal expectations. Death masks have become a popular literary device used to explore the themes of death and dying, and their use has contributed significantly to the development of literature.

The Masters Behind the Masks

The people who made death masks came from various professions and had different relationships with the deceased. The relationship between the maker of the death mask and the deceased varied depending on the circumstances. In ancient times, the maker of the death mask may have had no personal connection to the deceased, but rather was commissioned by someone who wanted to honor the deceased's memory.

During the Renaissance period, the maker of a death mask may have been a personal friend or patron of the deceased, who wanted to create a lasting tribute to their memory.

In more recent times, the maker of the death mask is often a professional who may or may not have a personal relationship with the deceased, but nevertheless is responsible for creating an accurate representation of their face. Below is a list of some of the more notable people who made death masks:

Jean-Antoine Houdon:

Jean-Antoine Houdon was an 18th-century French sculptor known for his portraits of notable figures such as George Washington, Benjamin

Franklin, and Voltaire [11]. Houdon believed that death masks were an important tool for capturing the true likeness of a person and preserving their memory.

Madame Tussaud:

Madame Tussaud, born as Anna Maria Grosholtz, was a 19th-century French artist and entrepreneur who became famous for her wax sculptures of celebrities and historical figures [12]. She learned the art of wax modeling from her mentor Dr. Philippe Curtius, who also taught her the technique of creating death masks.

She created death masks of famous figures such as Louis XVI, Marie Antoinette, and Robespierre during the French Revolution, which were used as political propaganda. After moving to London, she continued to create death masks of notable figures such as Lord Nelson and William Pitt the Younger. Madame Tussaud's skill in creating lifelike wax figures, including death masks, helped establish her as a successful artist and entrepreneur, and her wax museums remain popular tourist attractions to this day.

James De Ville:

He was a British phrenologist and mask-maker in the 19th century that was known for his expertise in creating death masks [13]. De Ville believed that death masks could provide valuable insights into a person's character and mental faculties, as he was also a proponent of phrenology, the study of the shape and size of the human skull as an indicator of a person's mental and moral traits. De Ville created death masks of notable figures such as William Wordsworth, John Keats, and Sir Isaac Newton, as well as less famous individuals.

Thomas Woolner:

A 19th-century British sculptor and poet, Thomas Woolner was a member of the Pre-Raphaelite movement [14]. He is known for his detailed and realistic sculptures, often featuring religious or mythological themes. Woolner also created a number of death masks throughout his career. He believed that death masks were an important tool for capturing the essence of a person and preserving their memory. Woolner created death masks of notable figures such as Charles Dickens, John Keats, and William Blake, among others.

Carlo Bartolomeo Rastrelli:

Rastrelli was an 18th-century Italian architect known for his contributions to the Baroque architecture style [15]. In addition to his work on buildings and palaces, Rastrelli was also known for his creation of death masks. Rastrelli created death masks of prominent individuals, including members of royalty, and his skill in this area was highly regarded. His death masks were considered highly accurate and were often used as a means of preserving the memory of the deceased.

Franz Xaver Messerschmidt:

A German-Austrian sculptor born in 1736, he is famous for his creation of highly detailed and realistic death masks [16]. He was noted for capturing the features of the deceased in a way that allowed them to be remembered long after they had passed away. His work was widely popular during his lifetime, and he was considered one of the greatest sculptors of his time. However, he also suffered from mental illness and began creating bizarre and grotesque sculptures of distorted faces. Despite this, his death masks continue to be highly valued as works of art and historical artifacts.

Count Joseph Deym von Stritetz:

According to legend Count Joseph Deym von Stritetz made a death mask of Mozart [17]. The mask supposedly went to Mozart's widow, but disappeared sometime after. Stritetz was an Austrian nobleman who is known for his passion for creating death masks. He became interested in this art form after seeing a mask of Napoleon Bonaparte and began collecting them. Deym even developed his own method of creating the masks. His collection of death masks became famous and was eventually acquired by the Kunsthistorisches Museum in Vienna.

Domenico Brucciani:

He was an Italian sculptor and founder of the Brucciani & Co. firm in London. He was known for his expertise in the field of death masks [18]. Brucciani's death masks were sought after by museums, collectors, and individuals as a way to preserve the memory of notable figures such as Charles Dickens, Charles Darwin, and Queen Victoria. His reputation for accuracy and attention to detail earned him commissions from institutions across Europe, including the British Museum and the Louvre.

Nick Reynolds:

Reynolds was an American artist and founder of the Forensic Science Institute in California [19]. He gained worldwide recognition for his expertise in the field of death masks. His death masks were used for both identification purposes and as artistic expressions. Reynolds worked with law enforcement agencies and museums to create accurate depictions of notable historical figures, including Abraham Lincoln, Napoleon Bonaparte, and Beethoven. He also created death masks for victims of major disasters such as the San

Francisco earthquake of 1906 and the Titanic sinking. He also created death masks for people as diverse as punk icon Malcolm McLaren and Hollywood legend Peter O'Toole. Reynolds contribution to the field of death masks has left a lasting impact on the history of forensic science and art.

Famous Death Masks

Royalty & Nobility

King Henry IV of France:

Fig 5

King Henry IV of France, also known as Henry of Navarre, was born on December 13, 1553, in Pau, Navarre, France [20]. He was the son of Antoine de Bourbon, Duke of Vendome and Jeanne d'Albret, Queen of Navarre. Henry was the king of Navarre from 1572 and the king of France from 1589 to 1610. He was the only French king to keep the Protestant faith and had to fight against the Catholic League, which denied that he was the rightful king of France.

Henry IV's reign was marked by a period of reconstruction and reconciliation after years of war and religious conflict. He implemented various reforms, including the Edict of Nantes, which granted religious tolerance to Protestants and brought a degree of stability to the country. He also made significant economic and infrastructure improvements, promoting trade, agriculture, and industry.

Henry IV faced numerous assassination attempts during his reign, as well as military conflicts with neighboring countries such as Spain. He was assassinated on May 14, 1610, by François Ravaillac, a Catholic zealot who stabbed him in the Rue de la Ferronnerie in Paris. Henry's coach was stopped by Ravaillac, who jumped on the running board and stabbed the king several times. Henry died shortly after the attack. His death alarmed the Protestants who feared that the Catholic League would take over the country.

A bust of Henry in wax, which is preserved at Chantilly, was proved to be the work of Italian sculptor G. Dupré. According to historian Malherbe, Dupré went to the Louvre the day after the king's death to make the wax effigy for his funeral, and took with him the modeler, who made a cast from the king's features. Henry was buried at the Saint Denis Basilica.

Marie Louise Gonzaga:

Fig 6

Marie Louise Gonzaga was born on August 18, 1611, in Nevers, France. She was the daughter of Charles I, Duke of Mantua and Montferrat, and Catherine of Mayenne [21]. Marie Louise was a member of the House of Gonzaga, one of the most powerful families in Italy. She was raised in a Catholic family and was educated in the arts, literature, and music.

Marie Louise Gonzaga was betrothed to and married Ladislaus IV Vasa, King of Poland and Grand Duke of Lithuania, in Paris in 1646. Ladislaus IV Vasa died in 1648, making Marie Louise a widow at the age of 37. She was remarried to his younger brother, John II Casimir, who became King of Poland and Grand Duke of Lithuania in 1649.

Gonzaga was known for her intelligence, beauty, and political acumen. She was a patron of the arts and supported many artists and writers of her time. Her husband, John II Casimir, was known for his piety and was not considered cruel or unfaithful. However, Marie Louise did forbid the servants and guards to call for her husband when she was lying on her deathbed, as he was busy taking part in one of the important Polish ceremonies. This may suggest that she was not particularly close to her husband at the end of her life.

Marie Louise died on May 10, 1667, at the age of 55. She was buried in the Wawel Cathedral in Kraków, Poland. After her death, a death mask was made of her face. The death mask is now in the collection of the National Museum in Warsaw,

Poland. The mask is made of wax and is painted to look like Marie Louise's face. It is a haunting reminder of the queen's life and legacy.

Queen Elizabeth I of England:

Fig 7

Queen Elizabeth I was one of England's most iconic monarchs, ruling from 1558 until her death in 1603 [22]. She was the daughter of King Henry VIII and his second wife, Anne Boleyn. Elizabeth was born on September 7, 1533, at Greenwich Palace in London. Her mother was executed when Elizabeth was just two years old, and she was declared illegitimate and removed from the line of succession. However, when her half-sister Mary I died in 1558, Elizabeth became queen.

Elizabeth's reign was marked by several major events, including the defeat of the Spanish Armada in 1588, which solidified England's position as a major world power. She was also known for her patronage of the arts, which led to a flourishing of literature, theater, and music in England during her reign.

In her later years, Elizabeth faced several challenges, including the threat of assassination plots and increasing pressure to name a successor. She famously never married and did not have any children, which led to a succession crisis upon her death. The crown eventually passed to James VI of Scotland, who became James I of England. James was the son of Mary, Queen of Scots, who was Elizabeth's cousin and former rival.

Elizabeth died on March 24, 1603, at Richmond Palace, London, at the age of 69. Her death was attributed to pneumonia, and she was buried in Westminster Abbey. A death mask was created by Maximilian Colt and was used to create a wax effigy of the queen for her funeral. The mask is now part of the collection at Westminster Abbey. Another death mask of Elizabeth was made in the early 20th century and is now held by the Royal Collection Trust. This mask shows Elizabeth with curled hair, an open ruff, a pearl necklace, and a jeweled bodice.

In recent years, artists have used Elizabeth's death mask as inspiration for their work. In 2018, artist Mat Collishaw created a hyper-realistic, animatronic mixed media installation called "The Mask of Youth." The installation depicted what Elizabeth may have looked like in her youth, based on the death mask and other historical sources. The installation is displayed at Queen's House in Greenwich, England.

King Charles XII of Sweden:

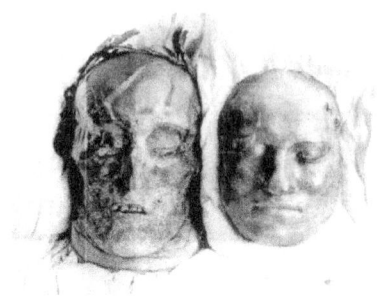

Fig 8

Charles XII, also known as Karl XII, was a Swedish king who reigned from 1697 until his death in 1718. He was born on June 17, 1682, in Stockholm, Sweden, and was the son of King Charles XI. At the age of 15, Charles XII became the monarch, following his father's death in April 1697.

After his father's death, Charles XII had to take on the burden of absolute kingship. Sweden was the victim of a concerted attack, and Charles's responsibility in planning and executing armed operations constantly increased, so that from 1702 he became the superior of most of his officers. Also from 1702, he began to take a greater part in the administration of the country. He was a skilled military strategist and a brave soldier, but his military campaigns were often reckless and costly. His invasion of Russia was a disaster, and he was forced to flee to Turkey in 1709.

On November 30, 1718, Charles XII died in the Swedish camp outside Fredriksten Fortress in

Norway. He was shot in the head by a bullet that went through his left temple and exited through his right [23]. The circumstances surrounding his death are still unclear, and there have been many theories put forth over the years. Some historians believe that he was killed by a stray bullet, while others speculate that he was assassinated.

After Charles XIIs death a mask was made of his face. His death mask is one of the most famous in Sweden, and it has been the subject of much study and analysis over the years. The mask shows the king's face in repose, with closed eyes and a peaceful expression.

Alexander I of Russia:

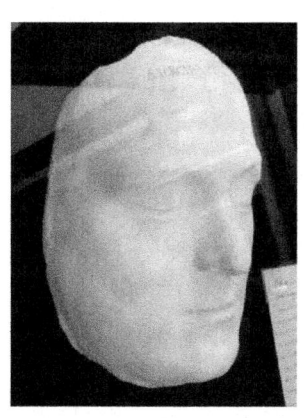

Fig 9

Tsar Alexander I of Russia was born on December 23, 1777, in St. Petersburg, Russia, and died in 1825, in Taganrog, Russia, at the age of 47. He was the eldest son of Emperor Paul I and Sophie Dorothea of Württemberg. He came to the throne in 1801 after his father was assassinated. He initiated the Napoleonic Wars, which led to Russia's victory over France and the expansion of its territory. However, after the defeat of Napoleon in 1815, Alexander I became increasingly disillusioned with politics and withdrew from public life [24].

Alexander I was a complex figure with a desire for reform and a strong sense of duty. He was a patron of the arts and sciences, and he founded the Russian Academy of Sciences. He also established the first public library in Russia and supported the development of the Russian theater.

His death remains one of the great mysteries of Russian history. On December 1, 1825, he was found dead in his bedchamber in the Winter Palace in St. Petersburg. The official cause of death was listed as typhus, but many believed that he was murdered by poisoning. His death mask, which was made shortly after his death, has been the subject of much fascination and speculation.

There is some discrepancy and debate about who actually made the death mask. Some sources attribute it to Marie-Anne Collot, a French sculptor who had worked with the tsar on other projects. Others credit it to François-Frédéric Lemot, another French sculptor who was known for creating death masks of notable figures. It's possible that both artists were involved in creating the mask, with Collot making the wax mold and Lemot producing the final plaster cast.

Mary Queen of Scots:

Fig 10

Mary, Queen of Scots was born on December 8, 1542, in Linlithgow Palace, Scotland. She became queen when her father, James V, died six days after her birth. Mary was sent to France to be raised at the court of the French king Henry II and was married in 1558 to his son Francis II. After Francis's brief rule as king ended with his premature death, Mary returned to Scotland in 1561. She was distrusted because of her Catholic upbringing and became a victim of intrigue among the Scottish nobles after marrying her ambitious cousin Henry Stewart (or Stuart), Lord Darnley, in 1565. After the birth of her son James in 1566, Mary faced many challenges, including opposition from the Protestant Church of Scotland and a rebellion by her husband, who was eventually murdered in 1567. Mary then married the Earl of Bothwell, who was suspected of the murder, and faced a revolt by the Scottish nobility. She fled to England, hoping to gain the protection of her cousin Elizabeth I, but was imprisoned instead.

Mary was accused of plotting to assassinate Elizabeth and sentenced to death. Her trial took place from October 14-15, 1586, shortly after she had been implicated in the Babington Plot, a plot led by Roman Catholic nobleman Anthony Babington, when letters said to be from Mary were intercepted [25]. These letters sanctioned the assassination of Elizabeth I, allowing Mary to be put on trial. She was found guilty and executed at the age of 44 on the orders of Elizabeth I of England on February 8, 1587, at Fotheringhay Castle in Nottinghamshire. Mary was accompanied to the scaffold by her pet dog that refused to leave her side even after her death.

After her execution, Mary's clothes were burned so they could not be kept as relics. Her embalmed body was hidden at Fotheringhay for six months then buried in a secret ceremony at Peterborough Cathedral. A mold made of plaster was taken of Mary's face after her execution and several casts were made from the mold. One of Mary's death masks is on display at the National Museum of Scotland in Edinburgh. The mask is a haunting reminder of Mary's tragic end.

Frederick the Great:

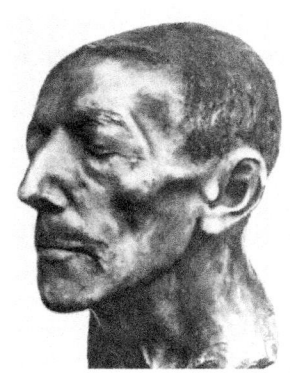

Fig 11

Frederick II, also known as "Frederick the Great," was a Prussian king who reigned from 1740 until his death in 1786. He is remembered as one of the most famous and successful monarchs in Prussian and German history, leading the country to prominence in Europe and introducing significant reforms in the government, the economy, and the military [26].

Frederick was born in Berlin in 1712 and was the eldest son of King Frederick William I. He received a strict and disciplined education that emphasized military training. After his father's death, Frederick ascended to the throne in 1740, and immediately embarked on a series of military campaigns that solidified Prussia's position as a major power in Europe. He was a brilliant military strategist and led Prussia to victory in several wars, including the War of the Austrian Succession and the Seven Years' War. He was also a patron of the arts and sciences and established the Berlin Academy of Sciences. He was also a prolific writer and composed several works on military strategy, politics, and philosophy.

Despite his achievements, Frederick faced several challenges during his reign, including wars, economic crises, and political opposition. He also suffered from health problems, such as gout, rheumatism, and depression, which affected his ability to rule effectively in his later years. Frederick died on August 17, 1786, at the age of 74, in his palace in Potsdam.

The death mask of Frederick the Great, created by Johann Christoph Friedrich von Eckstein, is known for its accuracy and realism, and is considered to be one of the most iconic and recognizable death masks in history. Frederick had a prominently hooked nose and little else to make him look handsome. This aquiline nose is not depicted in the official painted portraits of him, which are idealized and do not reflect how he looked according to his death mask. Since his death the mask has been used as a model for countless sculptures, portraits, and other depictions of the king, and is a valuable artifact that offers a unique glimpse into the life and legacy of one of the most important figures in German history.

Louise of Prussia:

Fig 12

Louise of Prussia was born on March 3, 1776, in Hanover, Germany. She was the daughter of Prince Charles of Mecklenburg-Strelitz and Princess Friederike of Hesse-Darmstadt. Louise grew up in a cultured and educated family and received an excellent education in literature, music, and art [27].

Louise was known for her intelligence, charm, and beauty. She was also an advocate for social reform and education, particularly for women. She founded several schools and supported the development of women's education, which was a rare initiative at the time.

Louise played an important role in the Prussian court, and was known for her political influence. She was a strong advocate for peace, and tried to prevent the outbreak of war between Prussia and France. In 1806, Prussia was defeated by Napoleon Bonaparte's army, and Louise became a symbol of Prussian resistance. During the war, Louise used her position as Queen to rally support for the Prussian cause and visited hospitals to tend to wounded soldiers.

Tragically, Louise's health began to decline in 1810 and she died on July 19 of the same year at the age of 34, in the palace of Hohenzieritz. Her death was a great loss to Prussia, and she was mourned by her husband, her children, and her subjects. Her death mask was created by the sculptor Christian Philipp Wolff right after her death. The original mask is now located in the Schinkel Pavillon at Schloss Charlottenburg in Berlin, Germany, which is part of the Stiftung PreuBische Schlosser und Garten Berlin-Brandenburg.

King Henry VII of England:

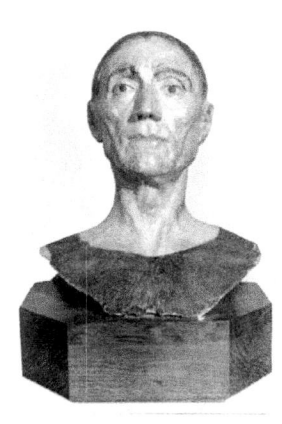

Fig 13

Henry VII was born on January 28, 1457, in Pembroke Castle, Pembrokeshire Wales. He was the son of Edmund Tudor, Earl of Richmond, and Margaret Beaufort. His father died before he was born, and his mother was in her early teens at the time [28].

In 1485, Henry landed in England with a small army and defeated King Richard III at the Battle of Bosworth Field, becoming king of England. Henry was the last king of England to win his throne on the field of battle. He married Elizabeth of York, the daughter of King Edward IV, in 1486, thus uniting the Houses of Lancaster and York and ending the Wars of the Roses. During his reign, Henry VII strengthened the monarchy, creating a powerful central government, establishing the Court of Star Chamber, and reforming the financial system.

His reign was marked by a successful area of policy, both in terms of efficiency and as a method of reducing the corruption endemic within the nobility of the Middle Ages. He was also known for his frugality and his ability to raise money through taxation. In 1502, Henry VII's life took a difficult and personal turn in which many people he was close to died in quick succession. His first son and heir apparent, Arthur, Prince of Wales, died suddenly at Ludlow Castle, very likely from a viral respiratory illness known at the time as the "English sweating." This was followed by the death of his wife, Elizabeth of York, in 1503, and his mother, Margaret Beaufort, in 1509. Henry VII was shattered by the loss of Elizabeth, and her death impacted him severely.

On April 21, 1509, Henry VII died at Richmond Palace at the age of 52. According to reports, his last days were far from peaceful, and he spent them in confession, prayer, weeping, and trying to bargain with God. The death mask of King Henry

VII was cast shortly after his death. The mask was made of wax and was used to create a likeness of the king for his tomb. In 2020, graphic artist Matt Loughrey produced a highly detailed digital replica of the face of King Henry VII from his death mask. Loughrey used photogrammetry software to build a digital model of the king's face. The project added significant detail and natural colors to the molded mask impression, transporting a long-dead face from the distant past into the present. The digital replica offers a glimpse of how the monarch may have looked in life.

Military Leaders

Henry Warner Slocum:

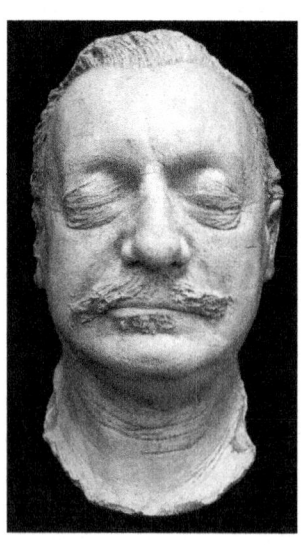

Fig 14

Henry Warner Slocum was a Union general during the American Civil War and later served in the United States House of Representatives. He was born on September 24, 1827, in Delphi, New York. Slocum graduated from the United States Military Academy at West Point in 1852 and served in the Seminole Wars in Florida [29]. He resigned from the army in

1856 and became a lawyer in Syracuse, New York. However, he rejoined the army when the Civil War broke out, and served as a major general of volunteers from 1862.

During the Civil War, Slocum fought in numerous major battles in the Eastern Theater, Georgia, and the Carolinas. He was one of the youngest major generals in the Army during the war. Slocum played a key role in the Battle of Gettysburg in 1863, where he commanded the right wing of the Army of the Potomac. He later led the Army of Georgia during General William Tecumseh Sherman's march to the sea in 1864.

After the war, Slocum served as a U.S. Representative from New York from 1869 to 1873. He was also a member of the New York State Assembly from 1874 to 1876. Slocum died on April 14, 1894, from heart failure. He was 66 years old at the time of his death. He was interred at Green-Wood Cemetery in Brooklyn, where Gen. Fitz-John Porter also is interred.

Slocum's death mask is on display at the Military History Institute in Carlisle, Pennsylvania. The mask was donated to the center by Slocum's granddaughter in 1977.

G. R. Mirabeau:

Fig 15

Honoré Gabriel Riqueti, Comte de Mirabeau, was a prominent figure in the French Revolution and a renowned military leader [30]. Born on March 9, 1749, in Bignon, France, Mirabeau contracted smallpox at a young age, which left him disfigured for life. He had a difficult relationship with his father, who disapproved of him and sent him away to study. At the age of 15, he was sent to the military academy in Paris, but he was expelled after getting into a brawl. He then became an adventurer, employed sometimes as a hired pamphleteer, sometimes as a secret agent, and came into contact with Louis XVI's ministers.

Mirabeau hailed from an aristocratic background, but he became known as a voice for the people and a champion of their rights. He possessed a charismatic personality and was a gifted orator, able to captivate audiences with his passionate speeches. Mirabeau's early political career was tumultuous, marked by conflicts with his father and clashes with the French monarchy due to his outspoken views.

He was elected to the Third Estate in 1789 and became one of the leaders of the National Assembly. However, he died before the Revolution reached its radical climax. Mirabeau died of pericarditis on April 2, 1791 in Paris, France at the age of 42. His death was met with national mourning, as he was thought of as a national hero and a father of the Revolution. He received a grand burial and was the first to be interred at the Panthéon.

After his death, a mask was made to preserve a vestige of the most famous revolutionary of his time. The street was still full of people when the mask was made. Mirabeau's legacy is a subject of debate among historians. Some see him as a great leader who almost saved the nation from terror, while others see him as a venal demagogue lacking political or moral values, or a traitor in the pay of the enemy.

Oliver Cromwell:

Fig 16

Oliver Cromwell was an English soldier, statesman, and lord protector of England, Scotland, and Ireland during the Republican Commonwealth [31]. He was born on April 25, 1599, in Huntingdon, Huntingdonshire, England, to Robert Cromwell and his wife Elizabeth, daughter of William Steward. Cromwell led parliamentary forces in the English Civil Wars and is known for his invasion of Ireland, where his forces took the ports of Drogheda and Wexford, and killed some 3,500 people in Drogheda.

Forced into a difficult balancing act in the last years of his life, Cromwell became a somewhat melancholy and bitter man. He died on September 3, 1658, at the age of 59, a month after the death of his favorite daughter. His death was due to complications related to malaria and kidney stone disease.

Cromwell was known to have suffered from depression, which doubtless affected his manner and personality. As a leader, Cromwell was often temperamental. He was elected to Parliament in 1628 but dissolved it in 1629. He was also known for abolishing the British monarchy after the bloody conclusion of the English Civil Wars (1642-1651) and the execution of King Charles I of England.

Cromwell's death mask was created following his death, and a plaster cast of his face was made, which is now on display at the Museum of London. The death mask is the only known image of Cromwell.

After Cromwell's death, his body was given a public funeral at Westminster Abbey equal to those of the monarchs who came before him. However, in 1661, King Charles II ordered Cromwell's body to be exhumed, tried, executed, and exhibited before the citizens of London. Cromwell was posthumously convicted of high treason and his corpse was hanged and beheaded. His head was displayed on a spike for over 20 years before it was blown down during a storm.

Admiral George Dewey:

Fig 17

Admiral George Dewey was a renowned naval commander in the United States Navy, famously known for his victory at the Battle of Manila Bay. The rank of Admiral of the Navy was created in 1899 and awarded only once to George Dewey in recognition of his victory.

He was born on December 26, 1837, in Montpelier, Vermont. Throughout his career, Dewey was involved in several naval battles, including the Battle of Port Hudson during the American Civil War, where he was wounded in the foot. He retired from active service in 1917, having served his country for over 60 years. On January 16, 1917, he died at his home in Washington, D.C. at the age of 79.

Dewey's death came after a brief illness of only six days. Upon his passing, all flags were ordered to be half-masted and an impressive funeral was held in his honor. His death was a great loss to the United States Navy and the entire country. In his honor, the Navy named a ship after him, the USS Dewey, which was commissioned in 1900 and served during both World War I and World War II.

He was laid to rest in Arlington National Cemetery in Virginia on January 20, 1917. A mausoleum was built for him in Arlington National Cemetery after his remains were interred. However, in 1925, his widow had his remains transferred to the Bethlehem Chapel in Washington National Cathedral [32].

One notable aspect of Dewey's death was the creation of his death mask. The mask was made shortly after his death, but there are discrepancies as to who made it. One account says it was made by sculptor Edward Berge. Another says it was made by Ulric Stonewall Jackson Dunbar, also a sculptor. The mask captures the likeness of Dewey's face, including his distinctive beard and mustache. Although there are photographs of the death mask, it is unclear as to where it is currently housed.

Jozef Pilsudski:

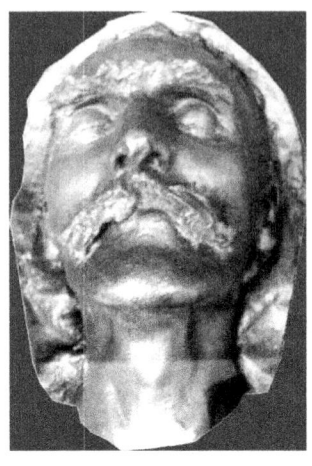

Fig 18

Józef Piłsudski was a Polish revolutionary and statesman who played a significant role in the establishment of the newly independent Poland in November 1918. He was born on December 5, 1867, in Żułów, Poland, which was then part of the Russian Empire [33]. Piłsudski studied medicine at Kharkov in 1885 but was suspended as politically suspect in 1886. In March 1887, he was arrested on a false charge of plotting the assassination of Tsar Alexander III and was banished to eastern Siberia for refusing to comply.

After his return in 1904, he began working for the socialists and became the leader of the Polish Socialist Party. Later, he became the most eminent representative of the "rebellious" generation and was in the ranks of the Riflemen and legionaries, where he strived to put Poland back on the map. He was the first chief of state of the newly independent Poland established in November 1918 and was also the leader of its armed forces. He held many political, military, and administrative positions, including Marshal

(1920 onwards), Prime Minister (1926-1928, 1930), and the de-facto leader of the Second Polish Republic.

He focused on military and foreign affairs until his death in 1935, developing a cult of personality that has survived into the 21st century. Although some aspects of Piłsudski's administration, such as imprisoning his political opponents at Bereza Kartuska, are controversial, he remains one of the most influential figures in Polish twentieth-century history and is widely regarded as a founder of modern Poland.

Piłsudski died on May 12, 1935, in Warsaw, Poland, at the age of 67. After his death, a death mask was made of his face, which is an unusual and interesting fact about his death. It was a common practice in the past to create death masks of famous people, and Piłsudski was no exception. The death mask of Piłsudski is now on display at the Józef Piłsudski Museum in Sulejówek, Poland.

Michael Collins:

Fig 19

Michael Collins was an Irish revolutionary leader, soldier, and politician born on October 16, 1890, in Clonakilty, Ireland. He played a key role in the fight for Irish independence from British rule in the early 20th century. Collins joined the Irish Republican Brotherhood (IRB) and Sinn Féin; two organizations dedicated to Irish independence, and quickly became an important figure in the movement. He was known for his strategic thinking, and as the chief planner and coordinator of the revolutionary movement, he organized numerous attacks on police and the assassination in November 1920 of many of Britain's leading intelligence agents in Ireland [34].

After the war, Collins played a key role in negotiating the Anglo-Irish Treaty of 1921, which established the Irish Free State. However, the treaty was unacceptable to de Valera and other republican leaders, and the civil war became inevitable. Collins was appointed as the commander-in-chief of the National Army during the Irish Civil War. On August 22, 1922, Collins was shot and killed in an ambush by anti-Treaty forces near Béal-na-mBlath, Cork, within a few miles of his birthplace. His death was a significant blow to the Irish Free State, and it marked a turning point in the conflict that was devastating Ireland.

His death mask, a plaster cast taken of his face after his death, has become an iconic symbol of his legacy. The mask was created by Dublin-based sculptor Seamus Murphy, who had worked with Collins previously on the creation of a memorial to the 1916 Easter Rising. Michael Collins' death mask is on display at the Cathal Brugha Barracks museum in Dublin. It was presented to the museum by Michael Collins' grandniece, Helen Collins. The Cathal Brugha Barracks museum is part of the National Museum of Ireland in Dublin, and the death mask is included in the permanent exhibition, Soldiers and Chiefs.

Ulysses S. Grant:

Fig 20

Ulysses S. Grant was an American military leader and politician who served as the 18th president of the United States from 1869 to 1877 [35]. He was born on April 27, 1822, in Point Pleasant, Ohio, and grew up in Georgetown, Ohio. His real name was Hiram Ulysses Grant, but due to a mistake by a congressman who nominated him to West Point, he was enrolled under the name Ulysses S. Grant, which he later adopted as his legal name.

Grant graduated from West Point in 1843 and served in the Mexican-American War. During the Civil War, he led the Union Army to victory over the Confederacy, serving as its commanding general from 1864 to 1865. After the war, Grant was elected as the 18th President of the United States, serving two terms from 1869 to 1877. He worked to implement Congressional Reconstruction and remove the vestiges of slavery. He also allowed Radical Reconstruction to run its course in the South, bolstering it at times with military force.

After retiring from the presidency, Grant became a partner in a financial firm, which went bankrupt. He went on a world tour and then returned to the United States to write his memoirs. However, he was diagnosed with throat cancer in 1884 and his health rapidly declined. He died on July 23, 1885, at his cottage at Mount McGregor, New York, at the age of 63.

After he died a death mask was made of his face. There are conflicting sources regarding who created the death mask. While some sources attribute the mask to sculptor Clark Mills others attribute it to artist/sculptor William Rudolf O'Donovan. The death mask of Ulysses S. Grant is now part of the collection at the Smithsonian National Museum of American History.

Robert E. Lee:

Fig 21

Robert E. Lee was a prominent figure in American history, known for his military leadership during the Civil War and his role in the Confederacy [36]. Born on January 19, 1807, in Stratford Hall, Westmoreland County, Virginia, Lee was the son of a Revolutionary War hero and a member of one of

Virginia's most prominent families. He attended the United States Military Academy at West Point, graduating second in his class in 1829. Lee served in the U.S. Army for over 30 years, including during the Mexican-American War, where he distinguished himself as a skilled tactician.

When the Civil War broke out in 1861, Lee was offered command of the Union army but instead chose to resign his commission and join the Confederate forces. He quickly rose through the ranks, becoming the commander of the Army of Northern Virginia and leading the Confederate forces to several early victories. However, the tide of the war eventually turned against the Confederacy, and Lee's army suffered a series of devastating defeats. Despite his military prowess, Lee was not able to overcome the Union forces, and in April 1865, he was forced to surrender to General Ulysses S. Grant at Appomattox Court House in Virginia.

After the war, Lee became the president of Washington College (now Washington and Lee University) in Lexington, Virginia. He worked to rebuild the school and promote reconciliation between the North and South. Lee died on October 12, 1870, from a stroke, and was buried in the Lee Chapel on the campus of Washington and Lee University.

A death mask was made of his face shortly after he died. Lee's death mask is particularly unusual because it was made by a former Confederate soldier named William Clark, who was also a dentist. Clark was present at Lee's deathbed and offered to make the mask as a way to honor the general. Lee's family agreed, and Clark made the mask using plaster of Paris. The mask was later used to create a bronze statue of Lee that stands in the U.S. Capitol building.

Pancho Villas:

Fig 22

Pancho Villa, originally named Doroteo Arango, was a Mexican revolutionary and guerrilla leader who fought against the regimes of both Porfirio Díaz and Victoriano Huerta. Born on June 5, 1878, in Hacienda de Río Grande, San Juan del Río, Durango, Mexico, Villa is known for his advocacy for the poor and land reform [37].

Villa's career as a revolutionary began in 1909 when he joined Francisco Madero's uprising against Mexican President Porfirio Díaz. He later became the leader of the División Del Norte, a group of rebels fighting against the government forces of Victoriano Huerta. Villa's military tactics were unconventional and included the use of hit-and-run attacks and ambushes. He was able to take control of the northern states of Mexico and successfully defeat Huerta's forces. Villa continued to fight against various other factions during the revolution and became embroiled in civil war in 1914.

Villa's life came to a violent end on July 20, 1923, in Parral, Chihuahua, Mexico. The specific conditions surrounding his death remain elusive, though it was likely connected to the ongoing feuds between Villa and his enemies. Villa was shot while driving his car and died instantly. His body was taken to a local funeral home, where his death mask was made. The death mask was later hidden at the Radford School in El Paso, Texas until the 1980s, when it was sent to the Historical Museum of the Mexican Revolution in Chihuahua, Mexico.

The death mask of Pancho Villa has been the subject of much debate over the years. Some people believe that the mask is a fake and that it was made long after Villa's death. Others believe that the mask is authentic and that it is an important historical artifact. The mask has been the subject of several legal battles. In the 1980s, the mask was sent to the United States for an exhibition, which caused controversy in Mexico. The Mexican government claimed that the mask was stolen and demanded its return and it was eventually returned to Mexico where it remains on display at the Historical Museum of the Mexican Revolution in Chihuahua. There is a plaster death mask of Villa in the collections of the El Paso Museum of History and another in the New Mexico History Museum. It is also possible that there are other death masks of Villa in different locations.

William Tecumseh Sherman:

Fig 23

William Tecumseh Sherman was an American soldier, businessman, and author, who played a crucial role in the American Civil War. He was born on February 8, 1820, in Lancaster, Ohio, to a family of prominent politicians. Sherman grew up in a family of 9 children, and his father passed away when he was just nine years old. After his father's death, he was raised by his mother and her family, who were influential in his upbringing. At 16 years old, his mother sent him to live with Thomas Ewing, who was a close family friend. Ewing was a United States senator from Ohio and would later serve as Secretary of the Interior under President Zachary Taylor.

Some sources suggest that Ewing adopted Sherman, while others indicate that he simply took him in as a ward.

Sherman was a gifted student, and he attended the United States Military Academy at West Point, where he graduated in 1840. Uneventful tours of duty in Florida, South Carolina, and Georgia resulted in the resignation of his commission at which time he turned, unsuccessfully, to banking and the law. He eventually returned to the military in 1861, at the outbreak of the Civil War.

During the Civil War, Sherman rose to prominence as one of the Union Army's most successful generals. He led several campaigns, including the Atlanta Campaign, which ultimately led to the Union's victory. His famous "March to the Sea" campaign, in which he led 60,000 troops on a 285-mile march from Atlanta to Savannah, Georgia, was one of the most significant events of the war. After the war, Sherman continued to serve in the military and was eventually promoted to General-in-Chief of the United States Army. He retired in 1883 and spent the rest of his life writing and traveling. Sherman died on February 14, 1891, in New York City.

A death mask of William Tecumseh Sherman was created by the American sculptor Daniel Chester French who was a prominent American sculptor best known for creating the statue of Abraham Lincoln at the Lincoln Memorial in Washington, D.C. [38]. He was a friend and admirer of William Tecumseh Sherman and was asked by Sherman's family to create the death mask after his passing. The resulting mask was then used as the basis for several posthumous busts of Sherman, including one that is on display at the Metropolitan Museum of Art in New York City.

François Athanase Charette:

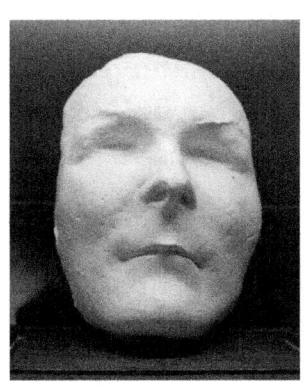

Fig 24

François de Charette de la Contrie was a French Royalist soldier and politician. He was born on May 2, 1763, and served in the French Navy during the American Revolutionary War before joining the counter-revolutionary forces [39].

Charette joined the revolt that began in the region of Nantes in March 1793 against the government of the Revolutionary National Convention. He fought in the royalists' siege of Nantes in June and July and the Battle of Torfu on September 19. However, he later quarreled with other rebel leaders and was arrested and imprisoned in Angers. He escaped from prison in January 1794 and resumed his leadership role in the royalist army.

Charette was known for his military prowess and was highly respected by his followers. He fought against the Revolutionary army and was able to capture several cities in the Vendée region. However, his luck began to change in 1795 when he was betrayed by his fellow Royalist leaders and was captured by the Republican army.

Charette was put on trial and was sentenced to death by a military tribunal on March 29, 1796. He was executed by firing squad the same day in Nantes, France, at the age of 32. After his death, Charette's face was covered with plaster to make a mold, which was used to create a death mask. The mask has been used as a model for sculptures and paintings depicting him. The death mask is now housed in the Musée Dobrée in Nantes, along with other artifacts related to the Revolt in the Vendée.

Charette's life and death have been depicted in various films and television shows. In the 2018 television series "La Guerre des As," he is the lead character, and his life story is depicted in the show.

Philosophers

Immanuel Kant:

Fig 25

Immanuel Kant was a German philosopher who lived from 1724 to 1804. He is considered one of the most important figures in modern Western philosophy and is known for his work in epistemology, ethics, and metaphysics. He was the fourth of nine children born to Johann Georg Cant, a harness maker, and Anna Regina Cant. Both of his parents were devout followers of Pietism, an 18th-century branch of the Lutheran Church. Later in his life, Immanuel changed the spelling of his name to Kant to adhere to German spelling practices.

Kant studied at the University of Königsberg and became a lecturer there in 1755. He spent most of his academic career at the university, eventually becoming a full professor in 1770. Kant's major works include *Critique of Pure Reason*, *Critique of Practical Reason*, and *Critique of Judgment*. These works are considered some of the most important in modern philosophy, and Kant is often credited with helping to establish the modern philosophical tradition.

He continued to write on philosophy until shortly before his death. In his last years, he became embittered due to his loss of memory [40]. He died on February 12, 1804, in the city of his birth, Königsberg, at the age of 79. His last words were "Es ist gut" (It is good) before expiring. His unfinished final work was published as *Opus Postumum*.

After his death, a death mask was made of Kant's face. The death mask is on display at the Königsberg State and University Library in Kaliningrad, Russia. The mask is a life-size replica of Kant's face, and it is said to be a very accurate representation of his features. The mask is made of plaster and is painted to look like Kant's skin. It is a fascinating artifact that gives us a glimpse into the physical appearance of one of the greatest philosophers of all time.

Friedrich Nietzsche:

Fig 26

Friedrich Nietzsche was a German philosopher, classical scholar, and cultural critic who became one of the most influential modern thinkers [41]. Nietzsche was born on

October 15, 1844, in Röcken, Saxony, Prussia. At the age of 24, he became a professor of classical philology at the University of Basel. Nietzsche's works are known for their criticism of traditional morality, religion, and philosophy.

Nietzsche's first book, *The Birth of Tragedy from the Spirit of Music*, marked his emancipation from the trappings of classical scholarship. Nietzsche's philosophy was characterized by his radical critique of truth in favor of perspectivism, a genealogical critique of religion and Christian morality, and a fondness for aphorism and irony.

One of Nietzsche's most famous works is *Thus Spoke Zarathustra*, in which he introduced the concept of the Übermensch or "superman," a person who transcends traditional morality and creates their own values. Nietzsche's ideas were controversial and often misunderstood during his lifetime, and he suffered from mental and physical health issues throughout his life. In 1889, he had a mental breakdown that left him unable to write or communicate for the rest of his life.

Nietzsche died on August 25, 1900, in Weimar, Thuringian States, at the age of 55. His death mask was created shortly after his death by artist Georg Brandes, who was a friend of Nietzsche's. The mask is now held in the Nietzsche Archive in

Weimar, Germany, and is considered to be one of the most accurate representations of Nietzsche's face. The mask has also been the subject of controversy, as some have claimed that it was altered to make Nietzsche look more Aryan, in line with the Nazi ideology that would later appropriate his ideas.

Giacomo Leopardi:

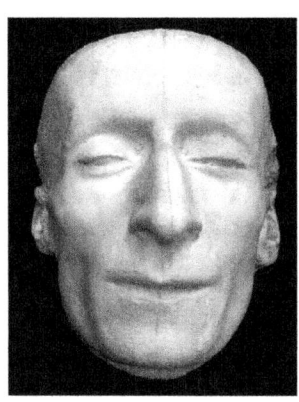

Fig 27

Giacomo Leopardi was an Italian philosopher, poet, and scholar, born on June 29, 1798, in Recanati, Papal States. He was a prominent figure in the 19th century, known for his outstanding philosophical and scholarly works, and superb lyric poetry. Leopardi's early life was marked by his love for learning and literature. He was a prodigious reader and writer, and by the age of 14, he had already written several poems and essays.

However, his life was also marked by personal struggles, including his frustrated love for his married cousin, Gertrude Cassi, and the death of Terese Fattorini, the young daughter of his father's friend, from consumption. These experiences robbed Leopardi of whatever optimism he had left, and he became increasingly disillusioned with life. In his later works, Leopardi's view of life became increasingly bleak. Life for Leopardi is an illusion, the only reality being death.

Despite his ailments, Leopardi continued to write and produce some of his most significant works, including *Operette Morali* (Moral Essays), which contains his most famous work, "Dialogue Between Fashion and Death" [42]. He also wrote several poems, including *The Infinite*, which has been hailed as one of the greatest works of Italian poetry.

Giacomo Leopardi died of heart failure in 1837 during a cholera epidemic in Naples. He was buried in the small church of San Vitale in Fuorigrotta, Italy. His lifelong sufferings included a broken heart, depression, and declining health. In addition, Leopardi's physical disabilities included a deformity in his spine and deteriorating vision, which led to the loss of sight in one of his eyes.

It is not known who created his death mask, but there is a plaster cast of the mask in the Lawrence Hutton Collection at Princeton University and possibly another is held in the Leopardi Museum in Recanati, Italy.

Jeremy Bentham:

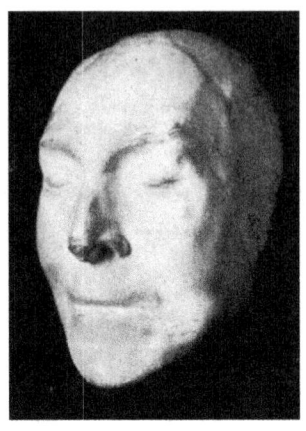

Fig 28

Jeremy Bentham was an English philosopher, economist, and theoretical jurist, considered the earliest and chief expounder of utilitarianism. He was born on February 15, 1748, in Houndsditch, London, into a wealthy family that supported the Tory party [43]. His father, Jeremiah Bentham, was a successful practitioner in the Court of Chancery, while his mother, Alicia Whitehorn nee Grove, was a pious woman.

Bentham was a child prodigy who began reading at the age of four and studying Latin at the same time. He went on to attend Oxford University at the age of 12, where he studied law. After completing his studies, Bentham began his career as a lawyer, but he soon became disillusioned with the legal profession and turned his attention to philosophy and political theory.

Bentham is most famous for his development of utilitarianism, a moral theory that holds that the best course of action is the one that maximizes the overall well-being of society. He believed that the value of an action should be judged based on its ability to produce happiness and reduce suffering. Bentham was a prolific writer, and his works include *An Introduction to the Principles of Morals and Legislation*, *The Panopticon*, and *The Book of Fallacies*. He was also a social reformer and advocated for prison reform, animal rights, and women's suffrage.

Bentham died on June 6, 1832, in London, at the age of 84. After his death, in accordance with his directions, his body was dissected in the presence of his friends and his head was preserved as a death mask. The skeleton was then reconstructed, supplied with a wax head to replace the original (which had been mummified), dressed in Bentham's own clothes, and set upright in a glass-fronted case. This was known as Bentham's "auto-icon," and it is currently on display at University College London.

Edmund Burke:

Fig 29

Edmund Burke was an Anglo-Irish statesman, economist, and philosopher born in Dublin on January 12, 1729. He served as a member of Parliament (MP) between 1766 and 1794 in the House of Commons of Great Britain with the Whig Party. Burke was a prominent political thinker and orator who played a significant role in the history of political theory. He was important in public life from 1765 to about 1795. Burke was a supporter of the American Revolution, but he opposed the French Revolution. He believed that the French Revolution would lead to chaos and anarchy, and he was critical of the enlightenment ideas that inspired it.

Burke's most famous work is *Reflections on the Revolution in France*, which he wrote in 1790. In this work, he criticized the French Revolution and argued that it would lead to the destruction of the social order. Burke believed that society was a complex organism that could not be easily changed without causing harm. He argued that the French Revolution was a threat to the stability of society and that it would lead to tyranny and oppression.

Burke's philosophy and political thought have continued to influence generations of thinkers and politicians in Great Britain, North America, and around the world. His legacy as a conservative thinker and defender of tradition and established institutions is still relevant today and has contributed to shaping modern conservative thought [44].

Burke's last years were clouded by the death of his son and the loss of many friends. He retired from Parliament in 1794 and died on July 9, 1797, at his home in Beaconsfield, Buckinghamshire, England. There is little information on the death mask of Edmund burke other than it is stated in the book *Portraits in Plaster* that it was made by the especial desire of Queen Charlotte on the day his death.

Poets, Novelists, & Writers

James Joyce:

Fig 30

James Joyce was an Irish novelist, poet, and short-story writer, born on February 2, 1882, in Dublin, Ireland [45]. He was the eldest of ten children and grew up in a middle-class family. Joyce was educated at Jesuit schools and later at University College Dublin, where he studied modern languages. He traveled to Trieste, Italy, where he worked as a language teacher, and later moved to Paris, France, where he befriended other modernist writers such as Ernest Hemingway and Sylvia Beach.

Joyce's most famous work is the novel *Ulysses*, which was published in 1922. The book is considered a masterpiece of modernist literature and is known for its complex narrative structure and use of stream-of-consciousness writing. Joyce's other major works include the novels *A Portrait of the Artist as a Young Man,* and *Finnegans Wake,* as well as a collection of short-stories *Dubliners.*

Joyce's life was marked by financial difficulties, health problems, and personal tragedies. He suffered from chronic eye problems and underwent several surgeries throughout his life. In 1941, he underwent surgery for a perforated ulcer in Zurich, Switzerland, where he had been living with his family. He died on January 13, 1941 from complications, less than a month before his 59th birthday.

After Joyce's death, a death mask was made of his face by sculptor Paul Speck in Zurich. The death mask is a plaster cast of Joyce's face and head, which captures his features and expression at the time of his death. The mask is now housed in the James Joyce Foundation in Zurich, along with other artifacts related to Joyce's life and work, such as his walking sticks, coins, and books.

Walt Whitman:

Fig 31

Walt Whitman, born on May 31, 1819, in West Hills, Long Island, New York, was an American poet, journalist, and essayist who is considered one of the most influential poets in American history [46]. He lived in Brooklyn as a child and left school at the age of 12, later holding various jobs, includeing writing and editing for periodicals. Whitman is best known for his collection of poetry called *Leaves of Grass*, which was first published in 1855 and is considered a landmark in American literature.

Whitman's life was marked by controversy. His poetry was often criticized for its frankness and sexuality. In 1856, he published a novel called *Franklin Evans; or The Inebriate*, which centers on a country boy who falls prey to drink in the big city and eventually causes the death of three women.

Throughout his life, Walt Whitman incorporated both transcendentalism and realism in his writings and is often referred to as the father of free verse. He aimed to transcend traditional poetic norms and mirror the potential freedoms found in America. Despite initially failing to garner popular attention for his poetry during his lifetime, Whitman's legacy has endured, and he is now recognized as the first writer of truly American poetry.

Whitman died on March 26, 1892, in Camden, New Jersey, at the age of 72. After Whitman's death, his friend Thomas Eakins and an assistant created his death mask as well as a plaster cast of the poet's face. On the day Whitman died, Eakins and Samuel Murray gathered all the necessary supplies to cast his face in plaster and early the next morning crossed the Delaware River to Camden to make the mold. The death mask of Walt Whitman from the Laurence Hutton Collection is the original as cast by Samuel Murray assisted by Thomas Eakins.

Whitman's funeral was held on March 30, 1892, at Harleigh Cemetery in Camden, New Jersey. The funeral was attended by a large number of people, including many prominent writers and artists of the time.

Kornel Makuszyński:

Fig 32

Kornel Makuszyński was a Polish writer born on January 8, 1884, in Stryj, which was then part of the Austrian Partition of Poland and is now in Ukraine [47]. He attended the Jan Długosz gymnasium in Lviv, Poland where he started writing poetry at the age of 14. Makuszyński had his first poem published while still in school. He went on to study law at the University of Lviv but did not complete his degree. Instead, he became a journalist and began writing children's books.

Makuszyński lived through World War II, and after the war, he settled in Zakopane, where he lived until his death. His time there was not easy, as he was blacklisted for a time after the war by Wincenty Rzymowski, a communist apparatchik and rival at the Polish Academy of Literature. Rzymowski was also a plagiarist. Makuszyński died in 1953 in Zakopane, where he was buried at the Peksowe Brzysko cemetery.

Makuszyński's death mask, which is a plaster or wax cast made of the face and head after death, is a part of his legacy. Makuszyński's death mask is currently held at the National Museum in Kraków.

Kornel Makuszyński's life and work have continued to be celebrated and appreciated long after his death. He is remembered as one of the most significant Polish children's book authors of the 20th century. His books have been translated into many languages, and his influence can still be seen in modern Polish literature.

Goldwin Smith:

Fig 33

Goldwin Smith was a prominent British historian, journalist, and social critic who played an active role in shaping public opinion during the Victorian era. He was a prolific writer, producing over thirty books on a variety of topics, including history, politics, religion, the history of England, the United States, and Canada. His writings were influential in shaping public opinion on issues such as Irish home rule, the Canadian confederation, and the role of the Anglican Church in society.

Smith was born in Reading, England, and received his education at Eton and Oxford University [48]. After completing his studies, he worked as a tutor, but soon found his true calling as a writer and journalist. He began his career as a journalist in 1852, writing for the Manchester Examiner and other newspapers. He soon became a regular contributor to the prestigious *Edinburgh Review* and the *Westminster Review*, two of the most influential literary and political journals of the time.

Smith's political and social views often put him at odds with the establishment, and he was not afraid to speak his mind. He was a vocal critic of the British Empire's policies in India and Africa, and he opposed the Boer War, which he saw as an unjust and imperialistic conflict. He also criticized the British government's treatment of the Irish, and he supported the cause of Irish nationalism. He was also a strong advocate for the rights of women and minorities, and he was involved in many political and social causes throughout his life.

Smith died in Toronto, Canada, in 1910, at the age of 87. His death was widely mourned, and he was remembered as one of the most influential writers and thinkers of his time. One unusual and interesting fact about Smith's death is that his death mask, a plaster cast of his face made after his death, was displayed at the University of Toronto until the 1970s. The mask was used by artists and sculptors as a model for portraits of Smith, and it was also used in scientific studies of facial features and expressions. However, the mask was eventually removed from public display because it was considered macabre and inappropriate. Today, the mask is kept in storage at the university's archives, and it is only shown to scholars and researchers by appointment.

Sir Walter Scott:

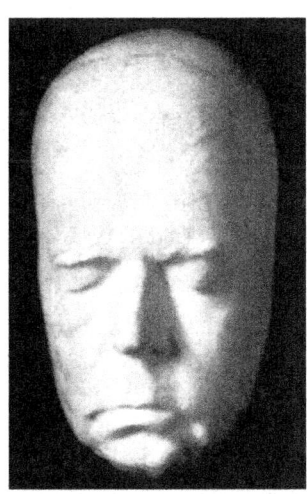

Fig 34

Sir Walter Scott was a renowned Scottish novelist, poet, historian, and biographer who is often considered the inventor and greatest practitioner of the historical novel. Scott was born in Edinburgh, Scotland, on August 15, 1771, to a farmer father and a mother who was fond of poetry and anecdotes [49]. From childhood, he was familiar with stories of the border region of Scotland. He studied law at the University of Edinburgh and was admitted to the bar in 1792, but he never practiced law extensively. Instead, he devoted himself to literature and became a successful writer.

Scott's literary career took off with the publication of his first novel, *Waverley*, in 1814. He went on to write many more novels, including *Ivanhoe*, *Rob Roy*, and *The Heart of Midlothian*. He also wrote poetry, including The "Lady of the Lake" and "Marmion." Scott's works were immensely popular and helped to revive interest in Scottish history and culture. Scott was also involved in politics and was a supporter of the Tory party. He was appointed as a Clerk of Session in 1799 and was made a Baronet in 1820. In 1826, he was appointed as the Sheriff of Selkirkshire.

Scott's health began to deteriorate in 1830, and he suffered a stroke in 1831 that left him partially paralyzed. Despite his declining health, he continued to work, completing his last novel *Castle Dangerous* in 1832. Scott died on September 21, 1832, at his home, Abbotsford, in Roxburghshire, Scotland, at the age of 61.

Sir Francis Chantrey, a Scottish sculptor, made Scott's death mask in the days immediately following Scott's death. The death mask of Sir Walter Scott is now held by the National Galleries of Scotland and is part of the Scottish National Portrait Gallery's collection.

Celia Thaxter:

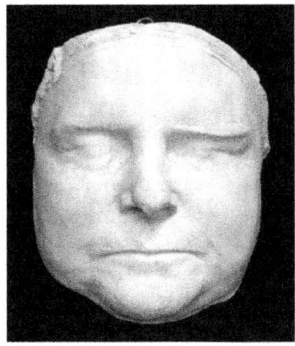

Fig 35

Celia Thaxter was a 19th-century American poet and writer born on June 29, 1835, in Portsmouth, New Hampshire. She was the daughter of Thomas Laighton, a lighthouse keeper and resort hotel owner, and his wife, Eliza. Celia spent most of her childhood on the Isles of Shoals, where her father was stationed. She was homeschooled by her mother and developed a love for literature and poetry at a young age. In 1851, at the age of 16, she married Levi Thaxter and moved to the mainland, where they had three sons.

Celia Thaxter's writing career began in the 1850s when she started publishing poems and essays in various magazines. Her first book, *Poems*, was published in 1872 and was well-received by critics. She went on to publish several more books, including *Driftweed* and *Among the Isles of Shoals*. Thaxter's love for the islands and ocean of her youth can be seen in her poetry and other writings, which were often centered on these themes. She was known as the "Island poet" and is regarded as one of the most important literary figures of her time [50].

Thaxter's life came to an end on August 26, 1894, when she died on Appledore Island, New Hampshire. Her death was due to a stroke, and she was buried on the island. After her death, a death mask was made of her face. It is unclear who made the mask, but a plaster cast of it does reside with the Lawrence Hutton Collection at Princeton University.

William Makepeace Thackery:

Fig 36

William Makepeace Thackeray was an English novelist, born on July 18, 1811, in Calcutta, India. He was the only son of Richmond Thackeray, an administrator in the East India Company, and Anne Becher. Thackeray was sent to England at the age of five to live with his aunt while he received his education. He studied at various schools in England, including Charterhouse School and Trinity College, Cambridge, but he did not complete his degree [51]. Thackeray studied law and art but soon became a prolific writer for periodicals, using a variety of pen names. He eventually became a successful novelist.

Thackeray's most famous works include *Vanity Fair* (1847-1848), a novel set in the Napoleonic period in England, and The *History of Henry Esmond, Esq.* (1852), set in the early 18th century. He also wrote *The Newcomes* (1855), *The Virginians* (1857-1859), and *The Adventures of Philip* (1862-1863). Thackeray was known for his satirical and humorous writing style, and his works often criticized the social and moral values of Victorian society.

Thackeray's health declined due to excessive eating, drinking, and lack of exercise. He died from a stroke on December 24, 1863, at the age of 52, which shocked his family, friends, and the reading public. According to the book *Portraits in Plaster*, the death mask of William Makepeace Thackeray was made by Brucciani on Christmas morning. It was cast in plaster and later used as the basis for a bronze bust. The plaster cast of Thackeray's death mask is held by the Victoria and Albert Museum in London.

Edward Kean:

Fig 37

Edward George Kean was an American television pioneer and writer. He was born in Manhattan on October 28, 1924. As a child, he started writing songs while at summer camp. Later he helped create the Howdy Doody children's TV show.

He served in the United States Navy during World War II and was based at Cornell University through the V-12 Navy College Training Program, and earned a degree from Columbia University.

Edward Kean was the chief writer of the Howdy Doody show, which was a popular children's television program in the 1950s. The show was broadcast live and featured a cast of puppets and human characters. Kean wrote over 2,000 episodes of the program, which aired from 1947 to 1960. He was responsible for creating many of the show's most memorable characters, including Howdy Doody himself, and was known for his ability to write for children. Kean's writing style was engaging and entertaining, and he had a talent for creating stories that would capture the attention of young viewers. After leaving the show, he wrote for other television programs, children's books, and did further work for Dell (comics and books).

Kean died at age 85 on August 13, 2010, at a health care facility in West Bloomfield Township, Michigan, due to emphysema [52]. He was survived by his wife, Vivian, as well as by a son and a stepdaughter. There is no information about who created his death mask, but it is part of the Lawrence Hutton Collection at Princeton University.

Torquato Tasso:

Fig 38

Torquato Tasso was an Italian poet born on March 11, 1544, in Sorrento, Kingdom of Naples (Italy). His father was an epic and lyric poet of considerable fame in his day and had been secretary in the service of Ferrante Sanseverino. Tasso's child-hood included stays in Naples, Rome, Bergamo, and Pesaro. At the age of 13, Torquato already enjoyed a reputation as a scholar and poet. He was sent to the University of Padua to study law, but he paid more attention to philosophy and poetry [53].

Tasso is best known for his 1591 poem "Gerusalemme Liberata" (Jerusalem Delivered), in which he depicts a highly imaginative version of the combats between Christians and Muslims at the end of the First Crusade during the siege of Jerusalem. The poem was a success, and Tasso gained immense popularity among his contemporaries.

The five years between 1565 and 1570 seem to have been the happiest of Tasso's life, although his father's death in 1569 caused his affectionate nature to turn melancholy. In 1575, he was invited to the court of Alfonso II d'Este, Duke of Ferrara, where he enjoyed a period of great creativity and happiness. However, his stay at Ferrara was not without its troubles. He fell in love with the Duke's sister, Leonora, and he was eventually sent to a hospital for the insane.

He was accused of madness and imprisoned for seven years in a mental hospital in Ferrara. The reasons for his confinement are unclear, but it is speculated that his mental breakdown was due to the pressure and stress he experienced as a courtier, and the intrigues and jealousies among his peers.

Tasso died in the monastery of Sant'Onofrio in Rome in April 1595, aged 51. He died a few days before he was to be crowned on the Capitoline Hill as the king of poets by Pope Clement VIII. The last twenty years of his existence had been practically and artistically unsatisfying. A death mask was made shortly after Tasso's death, but it is not clear whether it currently resides in the Palazzo Braschi Museum in Rome or the Museo di Roma. However, a plaster cast of his death mask is on display at the Countway Library of Medicine at Harvard University.

Samual Johnson:

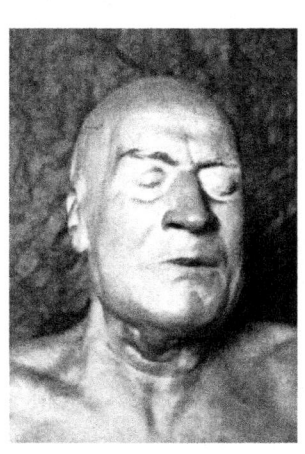

Fig 39

Samuel Johnson was an English writer, poet, and lexicographer who lived from 1709 to 1784. He is best known for his contributions to the English language, including his work on the first comprehensive English dictionary. Johnson was born in Lichfield, Staffordshire, England, and was the son of a bookseller. As a child, Johnson was often sick and had scrofula, a form of tuberculosis, which affected the appearance of his face and caused weak eyesight [54].

After attending a brief stint at the University of Oxford, Johnson moved to London after the failure of a school he tried to open. Johnson's early career was marked by poverty and struggle. He worked as a teacher and a writer, but his work was not successful. In 1735, he married a widow named Elizabeth Porter, who was more than 20 years his senior. She had three children from her previous marriage, and Johnson became a stepfather to them.

Johnson's literary career began to take off in the 1740s. He wrote a series of essays called *The Rambler*, which was published in a newspaper. He also wrote the play *Irene*, which was produced in 1749. However, his most famous work is the *Dictionary of the English Language*, which he began working on in 1746. The dictionary was published in 1755.

Johnson's later years were marked by illness and depression. He suffered from a number of physical and mental health problems, including gout, deafness, and anxiety. Johnson died on December 13, 1784, in London. A mold of his face was taken after his death, under the direction of Dr. Johnson's medical attendant, Mr. Cruikshanks. Although, is unclear as to who made the actual cast. This cast is commonly referred to as Johnson's death mask and is now held at the British Museum in London.

William Shakespeare:

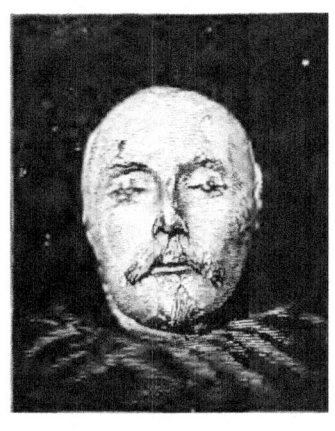

Fig 40

William Shakespeare was born in Stratford-upon-Avon, England, in 1564, and is widely regarded as one of the greatest playwrights in history [55]. Shakespeare's life is shrouded in mystery, and there are many gaps in our knowledge of his personal life. However, we do know that he married Anne Hathaway in 1582, and they had three children together.

He wrote over 38 plays and 154 sonnets, which are still performed and studied today. He is known for tragedies such as *Hamlet, McBeth,* and *King Lear;* comedies such as *A Midsummer Night's Dream,* and *Much Ado About Nothing;* histories such as *Henry V,* and *Julius Caesar.*

Shakespeare moved to London in the late 1580s and began working as an actor and playwright. He quickly became a popular and successful writer, and his plays were performed at the Globe Theatre, which he co-owned. Shakespeare's personal life was dealt a severe blow by the sudden death of his son Hamnet at the age of 11 in 1596. Despite this tragedy, Shakespeare continued on to become a celebrated playwright, eventually becoming a favorite of Queen Elizabeth and King James.

Shakespeare died on April 23, 1616, in his hometown of Stratford-upon-Avon. The exact cause of his death is unknown, but there are many theories. Some believe that he died of a fever, while others think he may have had cancer. There are even rumors that he was poisoned. However, there is no concrete evidence to support any of these theories. Shakespeare is buried at Holy Trinity Church in Stratford-upon-Avon. Despite the fact that Shakespeare was a celebrated figure in his time, his burial was modest, and his grave is not particularly ornate.

One interesting aspect of Shakespeare's death is that a death mask was made of him by a man named Dugdale, who was a friend of the playwright. There is some controversy about the authenticity of the death mask, as it was not discovered until the 18th century, long after Shakespeare's death. The mask is now on display at the Shakespeare Birthplace Trust in Stratford-upon-Avon, where visitors can see it for themselves.

Dante Alighieri:

Fig 41

Dante Alighieri was an Italian poet and philosopher born in Florence, Italy in May 1265 [56]. His family belonged to a noble but no longer wealthy lineage. Dante's education was typical of a youth of his time and social status. At the age of 12, he was betrothed to Gemma Donati, the daughter of a famous Florentine family.

Dante is best known for his epic poem *The Divine Comedy*, which consists of three parts: "Inferno," "Purgatorio," and "Paradiso." This masterpiece was written between 1308 and 1320. It tells the story of Dante's journey through Hell, Purgatory, and Heaven, accompanied by the poet Virgil. In his work, Dante used his poetic and philosophical talents to explore themes such as love, sin, redemption, and the human condition.

Dante was an active member of the Florentine political scene and became involved in the struggles between the Guelfs and Ghibellines, two rival factions that fought for control of the city. Dante supported the White Guelfs and served in several public offices, but his political career was cut short when the Black Guelfs, his opponents, seized power in 1302 and banished him from Florence for his political beliefs. He spent the rest of his life in various cities, including Verona, Bologna, and Ravenna.

Dante Alighieri died on September 13/14, 1321, in Ravenna, Italy. A copy of Dante's so-called death mask has been displayed since 1911 in the Palazzo Vecchio in Florence. Scholars today believe that it is not the true death mask. It is believed that Dante's original death mask was lost, and the mask on display is a later copy.

John Keats:

Fig 42

John Keats was a celebrated English Romantic poet who lived a short yet meaningful life [57]. He was born on October 31, 1795, in London, England, the oldest of four siblings. His parents were Thomas Keats, a stable manager, and Frances Jennings. Unfortunately, his father died in a horse-riding accident in 1804 when John was just nine years old. His mother remarried, and Keats and his siblings went to live with their grandmother. Keats attended school at Enfield, where he was encouraged in his literary aspirations by Charles Cowden Clarke, the son of the school's headmaster.

By age 21, Keats decided to focus entirely on poetry. In 1819, he wrote some of his most famous poems, including "Ode to a Nightingale," "Ode on a Grecian Urn," and "Ode on Melancholy." These poems are considered some of the greatest works of English Romantic poetry.

Keats's life was marked by tragedy and illness. His brother Tom died of tuberculosis in 1818. That same year, he met and fell in love with Fanny Brawne, but their relationship was short-lived due to Keats's failing health. He was diagnosed with tuberculosis in 1820, and his health deteriorated rapidly. He traveled to Italy in the hope that the warmer climate would improve his condition. However, his health continued to decline, and he died in Rome on February 23, 1821, at the age of 25.

After his death, his close friend Joseph Severn made a death mask of Keats's face. The death mask was later used as a model for a posthumous portrait of Keats, painted by Severn. The mask is currently housed at the National Portrait Gallery in London.

Samuel Taylor Coleridge:

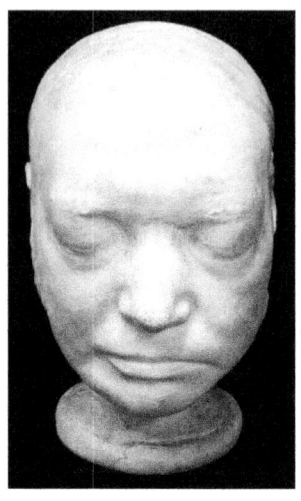

Fig 43

Samuel Taylor Coleridge was an English lyrical poet, critic, and philosopher who was born on October 21, 1772, in Ottery St. Mary, Devonshire, England [58]. After his father's death in 1782, he was sent to Christ's Hospital for schooling where he demonstrated an amazing memory and an eagerness to learn. He later studied at the University of Cambridge.

Throughout his adult life, Coleridge had crippling bouts of anxiety and depression. It has been speculated that he had bipolar disorder, which had not been diagnosed at the time. Coleridge also struggled with rheumatism and neuralgia. His was addicted to opium, which impacted his life and work, leading him to experience vivid dreams and hallucinations that he incorporated into his writing. In 1804, he moved to the Lake District to be closer to Wordsworth and his family, but his addiction continued to worsen, and he eventually separated from his wife and children and moved to London.

Coleridge's most famous work is *The Rime of the Ancient Mariner*, which tells the story of a sailor who has committed a crime against the life principle by slaying an albatross and suffers from torments, physical, and mental.

Coleridge died on July 25, 1834, at the home of Dr. James Gillman in Highgate, near London. His death was attributed to heart failure, likely caused by years of opium addiction and poor health. It is unclear who made Samuel Taylor Coleridge's death mask. However, the death mask is part of the Laurence Hutton Life and Death Mask Collection at Princeton University. Another is also on display at the National Portrait Gallery in London.

Friedrich Schiller:

Fig 44

Schiller was born in 1759 in Marbach, Germany. He grew up in a military family and attended military school, but he was never particularly interested in a career in the military. Instead, he was drawn to literature and began writing poetry and plays in his spare time. In 1781, he published his first play, *The Robbers*, which became an instant success and launched his career as a playwright.

In 1790, Schiller married Charlotte von Lengefeld, and the couple had two sons and two daughters together [59]. However, his health began to decline rapidly in the years following his marriage, and he struggled with a number of health issues. Despite his poor health, Schiller continued to write and publish prolifically, producing a number of famous plays and poems over the course of his career.

Schiller died on May 9, 1805, at the age of 45. The cause of his death was reportedly tuberculosis, which he had been suffering from for many years. After Schiller's death, a death mask was made of his face. The physical resemblance between the skull and the extant death mask, as well as to portraits of Schiller, had led many experts to believe that the skull was Schiller's. There is some controversy surrounding the final resting place of Friedrich Schiller, and whether or not his tomb is currently vacant. Schiller was initially buried in a cemetery in Weimar, Germany, but his remains were later moved to a mausoleum in the same cemetery in 1826. However, there are conflicting reports about what happened to his remains after that.

According to some sources, including the official website of the city of Weimar, Schiller's remains were removed from the mausoleum during World War II to protect them from damage. They were reportedly moved to a secure location and then returned to the mausoleum after the war ended. However, there are other reports that suggest that Schiller's remains were never returned to the mausoleum and that his tomb is currently vacant.

Heinrich Heine:

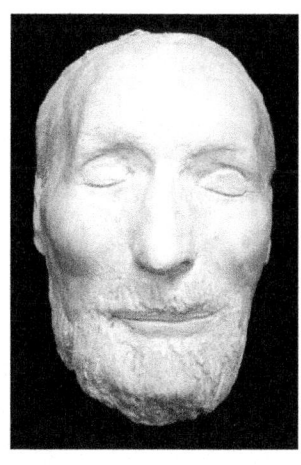

Fig 45

Heinrich Heine was a renowned German poet, writer, and literary critic, born on December 13, 1797, in Düsseldorf, Germany [60]. His birth name was Harry Heine, and he later changed it to Christian Johann Heinrich Heine. Heine came from an assimilated Jewish family, and his uncle supported him financially for much of his life. However, his uncle later wrote him out of his will, which caused him financial difficulties.

Heine's life was full of contradictions. He was a German poet who wrote in French, a Jew who converted to Christianity, and a liberal who was critical of the French Revolution. He was also a political activist who was critical of political activism. Heine was a controversial figure in his time, and his work was often censored. He was a vocal critic of German conservatism and was known for his satirical writing.

In 1827 he published his most famous work, *The Buch der Lieder* (The Book of Songs), which contained lyrics that were frequently set to music. Heine's poetry was highly influential, and he became well known internationally.

In the later years of his life, Heine's poetry became more somber and focused on his own mortality. In 1851, he moved to Paris, France, where he lived for the remainder of his life. Heine's death was a tragic one. He died on February 17, 1856, in Paris, France, at the age of 58. He had been bedridden for eight years due to a spinal disease, and his death was a relief from his suffering.

It is not clear who made Heine's death mask. However, it is known that Salman Schocken, a German-Jewish businessman and publisher, added Heine's death mask to his collection of Heine's works. This took place during Hitler's regime when Heine's books were burned by the Nazis. The death mask of Heinrich Heine is now part of the Laurence Hutton Collection at Princeton University.

Victor Hugo:

Fig 46

Victor Hugo was a French poet, novelist, and dramatist who is widely considered the most important of the French Romantic writers. He was born on February 26, 1802, in Besançon, France, to Sophie Trébuchet and Joseph Léopold Sigisbert Hugo [61]. Hugo's father was a general in Napoleon's army, and his mother was a devoted Catholic royalist who instilled in him a love for literature and the arts.

Hugo began writing at a young age and published his first book of poetry at age 20. He quickly gained recognition as an important figure in Romanticism with the publication of his verse "Drama Cromwell" in 1827. Over the course of his career, Hugo wrote numerous works of fiction, poetry, and drama, including *Les Misérables*, *The Hunchback of Notre-Dame*, and *Hernani*.

In later life, Hugo was a politician and political writer. He spent the years 1851–70 in exile for his Republican views, producing his most extensive and original works, including *Les Châtiments* (1853), poems of political satire; *Les Contemplations* (1856); and the first installment of *The Legend of the Centuries* (1859, 1877, 1883).

Victor Hugo died on May 22, 1885, in Paris, at the age of 83, from pneumonia. His death generated intense national mourning. He was not only revered as a towering figure in literature, but he was also a statesman who shaped the Third Republic and democracy in France. His last wishes were, "I leave 50,000 francs to the poor. I wish to be taken to the cemetery in the hearse customarily used for the poor. I refuse the prayers of all churches. I believe in God."

After his death, a mask was made of his face. Hugo's death mask is on display at the Maison de Victor Hugo, a museum in Paris dedicated to his life and work. The museum also has a collection of his personal belongings, manuscripts, and first editions of his works.

Carl Michael Bellman:

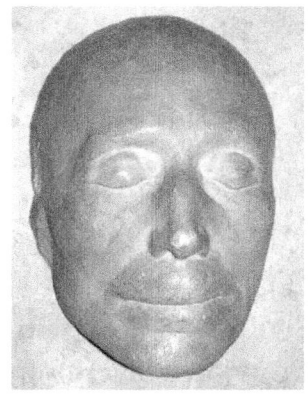

Fig 47

Carl Michael Bellman was a poet and musician born on February 4, 1740, in Stockholm, Sweden. His parents were not wealthy, and he was sent to school at the age of seven. He was a bright student and showed an early interest in music and poetry.

Bellman's most well-known works are the *Fredman's Epistles* and *Fredman's Songs*, which are still popular in Scandinavia today [62]. His poetry often included backanalistic themes and celebrations of wine and women, earning him the title "Nordens Anakreon." Bellman is considered one of Sweden's national poets and is little known elsewhere.

Bellman's life was marked by financial difficulties, and he struggled to make ends meet. He was often in debt and had to rely on the patronage of King Gustav III. Bellman's drinking and gambling habits did not help his financial situation, and he was often in trouble with the law. In 1794, Bellman was sued for debt by a man seeking revenge, knowing he was penniless. He owed a total of almost 4,000 Riksdaler. On February 11, 1795, he died in his sleep in his house in Gamla

Kungsholmsbrogatan (a street in Stockholm). He was buried in Klara churchyard with no gravestone, and its location is now unknown.

Bellman's death mask is a plaster cast of his face made after his death. It is now in the collection of the Swedish National Museum in Stockholm.

Jonathan Swift:

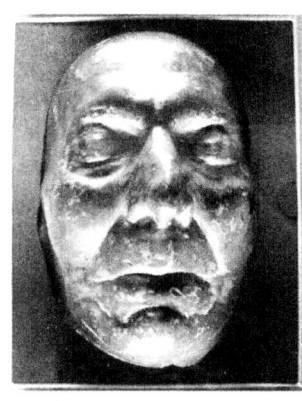

Fig 48

Jonathan Swift was born in Dublin, Ireland on November 30, 1667, to a poor family. His father, a noted clergyman in England died seven months before Jonathan's birth. There is not much known about Swift's childhood, and what is reported is not always agreed upon by biographers [63]. He was a student at Trinity College in Dublin during the anti-Catholic Revolution of 1688 in England. Swift was a Protestant, and the Irish Catholic reaction in Dublin led him to seek refuge in England. He worked as a secretary for Sir William Temple, a retired diplomat, and writer, and it was during this time that he began to write. Swift's first published work was a pamphlet titled "A Discourse on the Contests and Dissentions between the Nobles and the Commons in Athens and Rome," which was published in 1701.

Swift had a longtime love, Esther Johnson, whom he met when she was only eight years old. Johnson fell ill and died in January 1728, which moved Swift to write *The Death of Mrs. Johnson*. Swift is best known for his satirical works, including *Gulliver's Travels*, *A Modest Proposal*, and *A Tale of a Tub*. He is considered one of the greatest satirists and ironists in the history of the English language.

In 1742, Swift suffered from a stroke and lost the ability to speak. He died on October 19, 1745, and was laid to rest next to Esther Johnson inside Dublin's St. Patrick's Cathedral. A death mask was made prior to autopsy by applying plaster to his face to capture an exact likeness. It was probably taken within four hours of his death. The death mask is now held in the collection of the Trinity College Library in Dublin, Ireland.

James Hogg:

Fig 49

James Hogg, also known as the "Ettrick Shepherd," was a Scottish poet born on a small farm near Ettrick, Selkirkshire in 1770. His father, Robert Hogg, was a tenant farmer and his mother, Margaret Hogg, was known for collecting native Scottish ballads. Hogg spent most of his youth and early manhood as a shepherd and was almost entirely self-educated [64]. Despite his lack of formal education, Hogg became a successful poet during the ballad revival that accompanied the Romantic Movement. He wrote works such as *The Queen's Wake* and *Kilmeny* which gained him considerable reputation and popularity.

Hogg's life was marked by financial struggles, personal tragedies, and literary success. He married Margaret Phillips in 1820, and they had five children together. Hogg supported his family by working as a farmer and writing for various publications. He had a complicated relationship with the literary establishment of his time, including Sir Walter Scott and the publisher William Blackwood. Hogg's association with *Blackwood's Magazine* led to a falling out in 1821, but they reconciled shortly before Blackwood's death in 1834.

Hogg's death on November 21, 1835, was marked by a public outpouring of grief. He was buried in Ettrick Churchyard on November 27, 1835. The entry in the *Old Parish Register for Ettrick* gives his age at death as 65 and his residence.

A death mask was made shortly after his death and is on display in the courtroom of the old Sheriff Court in Selkirk. Another death mask is held in the collection of the National Galleries of Scotland. There is no information on who made the masks.

Scientists, Chemists, Physicists, & Doctors

Louis Agassiz:

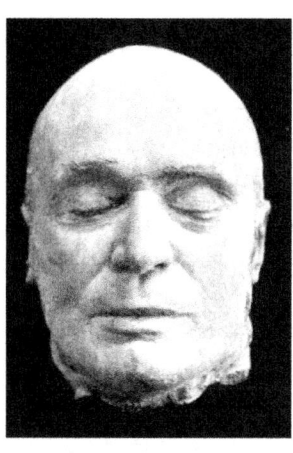

Louis Agassiz was a Swiss-American naturalist, geologist, and teacher who made revolutionary contributions to the study of natural science with landmark work on glacier activity and extinct fishes. He was born on May 28, 1807, in Motier, Switzerland, to a Protestant pastor.

Fig 50

In boyhood, he attended the gymnasium in Bienne and later the academy at Lausanne. He entered the universities of Zurich, Heidelberg, and Munich and took at Erlangen the degree of doctor of philosophy in 1829. In 1846, he moved to the United States, where he became a professor of zoology and geology at Harvard University. He achieved lasting fame through his innovative teaching methods, which altered the character of natural science education in the United States.

Agassiz's scientific achievements were extensive and encompassed various fields, including paleontology, glaciology, and zoology. He conducted groundbreaking research on fossil fish, making significant contributions to the understanding of ancient marine life. His work on glaciation provided crucial insights into the Earth's geological history, particularly in relation to the Ice Age. Agassiz's discoveries and theories greatly influenced the scientific community of his time and beyond [65].

In addition to his scientific pursuits, Agassiz was an exceptional teacher who inspired numerous students. He possessed a gift for imparting knowledge and had a profound impact on the development of American science education.

Agassiz was struck by ill health in the 1860s and resolved to return to the field for relaxation and to resume his studies of Brazilian fish. In April 1865, he led a party to Brazil. After his return in August 1866 an account of the expedition *A Journey in Brazil*, was published in 1868.

Agassiz died on December 14, 1873, in Cambridge, Massachusetts, at the age of 66. There is not much information about who made Agassiz's death mask. Although, one source does indicate that it is now part of the collection of the Peabody Museum of Archaeology and Ethnology at Harvard University.

Arthor H. Compton:

Fig 51

Arthur Holly Compton was an American physicist who was born on September 10, 1892, in Wooster, Ohio. Compton grew up in a family of intellectuals and academics and developed a keen interest in science from an early age. He earned his bachelor's degree from the College of Wooster in 1913 and then went on to study at Princeton University, where he earned his PhD in physics in 1916 [66]. After completing his studies, Compton joined the faculty at the University of Minnesota and then later the University of Chicago, where he spent the majority of his academic career. While at Chicago, he made his groundbreaking discovery of the Compton Effect in 1923. This phenomenon demonstrated the particle nature of electromagnetic radiation. He shared the Nobel Prize for Physics in 1927 with C.T.R. Wilson of England for this discovery.

Compton made significant contributions to the field of physics. He developed a theory of the intensity of X-ray reflection from crystals as a means of studying the arrangement of electrons and atoms. He also worked on the Manhattan Project, which was a research and development undertaking during World War II that produced the first nuclear weapons. Compton was a member of the project's scientific advisory committee and played a key role in the development of the atomic bomb.

Compton died on March 15, 1962, in Berkeley, California, from a cerebral hemorrhage. He was survived by his wife and sons. One source mentions that the death mask of Compton is now part of the collection of the National Museum of American History in Washington, D.C. There is no mention as to who made the mask. There is also a bronze bust made from the mask in the Laurence Hutton Collection at Princeton University.

Sir Isaac Newton:

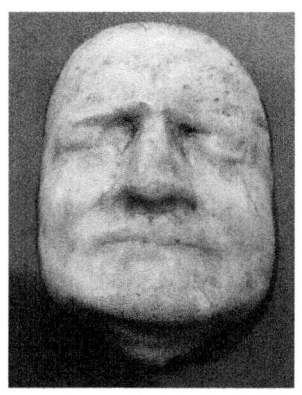

Fig 52

Sir Isaac Newton was an English physicist and mathematician who is widely regarded as one of the most influential scientists of all time. Newton was born on January 4, 1643, in Woolsthorpe, Lincolnshire, England. He was the only son of a local yeoman, also named Isaac Newton, who died three months before his birth.

Newton was educated at Cambridge University from 1661 to 1665, where he discovered the work of René Descartes. He was appointed Lucasian Professor of Mathematics at Cambridge University in 1669 and was elected a Fellow of the Royal Society in 1672. He continued his studies in mathematics and physics, publishing his first paper, "Method of Fluxions." He was a brilliant physicist and mathematician, who was the culminating figure of the Scientific Revolution of the 17th century. Newton's work laid the foundation for modern physics and astronomy.

Newton made many notable contributions to the field of science and mathematics throughout his lifetime. He is best known for his three laws of motion, which state that every object in a state of uniform motion will remain in that state of motion unless an external force acts on it; force equals mass times acceleration; and for every action, there is an equal and opposite reaction [67]. He published the laws in his book *Philosophiæ Naturalis Principia Mathematica* in 1687. He also developed the law of universal gravitation, which states that every point mass attracts every other point mass by a force acting along the line intersecting both points. This discovery helped to explain the motion of the planets and the stars.

When he was 80, he began to suffer from incontinence due to a weakness in the bladder, and his movement and diet became restricted. He ate mainly vegetables and broth and was plagued by a stone in the bladder. In 1725, he fell ill with gout and endured it until his death. Isaac Newton died in his sleep on March 20, 1727, in London, at the age of 84. He was given a ceremonial funeral, attended by nobles, scientists, and philosophers, and was buried in Westminster Abbey among kings and queens.

In 2008 a sample of hair that was kept by his descendants for over 300 years was found to contain mercury. This probably resulted from his alchemical pursuits. Mercury poisoning could explain Newton's eccentricity in late life. Newton's death mask, which was made shortly after his death, reveals what he really looked like. The nose appears to be the real deal, although it is slightly squished given the weight of the plaster. The mask is now on display at the Royal Society in London.

Alfred Nobel:

Fig 53

Alfred Nobel was a Swedish chemist, engineer, inventor, businessman, and philanthropist, born on October 21, 1833, in Stockholm, Sweden [68]. His family was impoverished, and Alfred Nobel's education was sporadic and informal. However, he became fluent in several languages and wrote poetry and drama. In 1842, Alfred moved with his mother and brothers to St. Petersburg, where his father had opened an armaments factory a few years prior. There, he trained as a chemical engineer, buttressed by post-graduate work in Sweden, Germany, France, and the United States.

He is best known for inventing dynamite and other more powerful explosives, as well as for founding the Nobel Prizes. Nobel was a complex personality who puzzled his contemporaries.

Although his business interests required him to travel almost constantly, he remained a lonely recluse who was prone to fits of depression.

Nobel's interests were reflected in the prize he established. He was interested in science, inventions, entrepreneurship, and philanthropy. He registered more than 350 patents in various countries, including patents for synthetic rubber, leather, and more. However, his most famous invention was dynamite, which he patented in 1867. Dynamite was a safer and more stable explosive than the nitroglycerin that was commonly used at the time. It was used in construction, mining, and warfare, and it made Nobel a wealthy man.

Nobel's complex personality and his involvement in the arms industry led to his decision to leave a better legacy after his death. In 1888, his brother Ludvig died while visiting Cannes, France, and a French newspaper mistakenly published an obituary for Alfred Nobel, calling him the "merchant of death." This incident is said to have brought about his decision to leave a better legacy after his death. In his will, he left the bulk of his fortune to establish the Nobel Prizes, which are awarded annually for achievements in physics, chemistry, medicine, literature, and peace.

Nobel died on December 10, 1896, in San Remo, Italy, at the age of 63. He never married and had no children. The death mask of Alfred Nobel is on display at the Nobel Museum in Stockholm, Sweden.

Joseph Leidy:

Fig 54

Joseph Leidy, born on September 9, 1823, in Philadelphia, was a highly esteemed American scientist-zoologist who made significant contributions to the fields of comparative anatomy, parasitology, and paleontology [69]. Leidy was a professor of anatomy at the University of Pennsylvania and later became a professor of natural history at Swarthmore College and the director of scientific and educational programs at the Wagner Free Institute of Science. He dominated vertebrate paleontology research in Florida during the latter half of the 19th century.

Leidy was the chief U.S. authority of his time on protozoa, and he published several works on the lower animal orders. One of his works, *Fresh Water Rhizopods of North America* (1879), became a standard work. In all, he published more than 600 works, among which are the *Elementary Treatise on Human Anatomy* (1861), recognized as a classic American text on the subject, and *On the Extinct Mammalia of Dakota and Nebraska* (1869), described by the prominent U.S. paleontologist.

Joseph Leidy died at home on April 30, 1891, in Philadelphia, Pennsylvania, at the age of 67. His death marked the end of an era for American science, as he was widely regarded as one of the most distinguished scientists of his time.

After Joseph Leidy's death, his nephew had a plaster mold made of his uncle's face. A death mask was created to preserve the likeness of Joseph Leidy and serve as a tribute to his memory. Copies of the death mask were presented to various institutions that Joseph Leidy had supported, including the College of Physicians, the Academy of Natural Sciences, and the American Philosophical Society.

Dr. John Hunter:

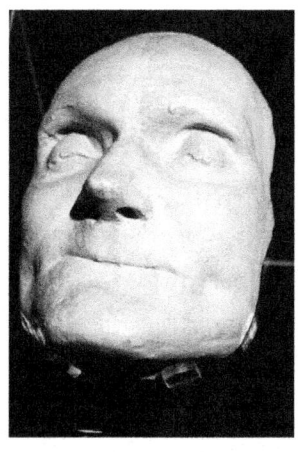

Fig 55

Dr. John Hunter was a prominent Scottish surgeon who is widely regarded as the founder of scientific surgery [70]. Hunter was born in Long Calderwood, Lanarkshire, Scotland, and he began his medical career as an apprentice to his elder brother William, who was also a surgeon. Hunter was also a teacher of, and collaborator with, Edward Jenner, pioneer of the smallpox vaccine.

Hunter's contributions to medicine were significant. He was the first to describe the lymphatic system and the first to perform a successful operation for aneurysm. He also made important contributions to the understanding of venereal disease, the treatment of gunshot wounds, and the study of teeth. Hunter was also known for his collection of anatomical specimens, which he used for research and teaching. His collection was eventually purchased by the British government and formed the basis of the Hunterian Museum at the Royal College of Surgeons in London.

One of the most controversial aspects of Hunter's legacy is his alleged acquisition of the body of Charles Byrne, a man who was nearly eight feet tall, and his subsequent study and exhibition of the body against Byrne's explicit wishes. Despite these ethical concerns, Hunter's work on Byrne's body was significant for its contributions to the study of acromegaly, a hormonal disorder characterized by excessive growth of the bones.

Hunter's death in 1793 was due to a heart attack brought on by an argument at St George's Hospital concerning the admission of students. He was originally buried at St Martin-in-the-Fields, but in 1859 was reburied in the north aisle of the nave in Westminster Abbey, reflecting his importance to the country.

A death mask of Dr. John Hunter exists and is housed at the Royal College of Surgeons of England. This mask is a first-generation copy of the original death mask that was made when Dr. Hunter died.

Blaise Pascal:

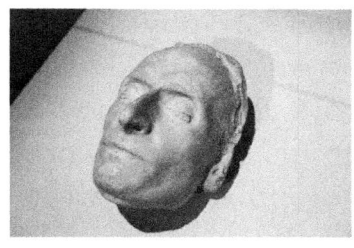

Fig 56

A French mathematician, physicist, religious philosopher, and master of prose, Blaise Pascal was born on June 19, 1623, in Clermont-Ferrand, France [71]. Pascal was a sickly child who suffered various pains and diseases throughout his life. According to a family anecdote related by his niece, at age one, he supposedly fell victim to a strange illness. His abdomen became distended and swollen, and the slightest annoyance triggered fits of crying and screaming. Despite his poor health, Pascal showed an early aptitude for mathematics, and by the age of 16, he had already made significant contributions to the field.

Pascal was known for his inventions, including the Pascaline, a mechanical calculator that could add and subtract, and his notable works, such as *Essai pour les coniques*, *Les Provinciales*, *Pensées*, *The Physical Treatises of Pascal*, and *Traité du Triangle Arithmétique*.

Pascal's most significant contributions to mathematics include laying the foundation for the modern theory of probabilities, formulating what came to be known as Pascal's principle of pressure, and developing Pascal's triangle. He also made important contributions to the study of conic sections and the cycloid. In physics, he conducted experiments on the weight and density of air and laid the groundwork for the study of hydrodynamics. In addition to his scientific work, Pascal was also a master of prose and wrote extensively on religious philosophy.

Pascal continued to suffer from poor health throughout his life. He died at the age of 39 on August 19, 1662, probably from carcinomatous meningitis following a malignant ulcer of the stomach. A mold of his face was made and used to create a bronze bust of Pascal, which is now on display at the Musée des Beaux-Arts in Rouen, France. Pascal's death mask is kept in the Musée des Lettres et Manuscrits in Paris and is a significant artifact of his life and death.

Composers

Ludwig van Beethoven:

Fig 57

Born in Bonn, Germany in1770, Beethoven displayed prodigious musical talent at a young age. He moved to Vienna in 1792 to study with Joseph Haydn, and he quickly established himself as a leading composer and performer in the city. He was known for his virtuosic piano playing and his innovative compositions, which pushed the boundaries of classical music. Beethoven's music was characterized by its emotional intensity, its use of unconventional harmonies and forms, and its powerful sense of drama.

Beethoven's personal life was often marked by turmoil and tragedy. His father was an alcoholic who frequently beat him and his siblings, and he struggled with his own health throughout his life. He began to experience hearing loss in his late twenties, and by the time he was in his forties, he was almost completely deaf. Despite this, he continued to compose some of his most important works during the last 10 years of his life when he was quite unable to hear [72].

Beethoven died on March 26, 1827, at the age of 56, following a prolonged illness. His death was witnessed by his sister-in-law, his secretary Karl Holz, and his close friend Anselm Hüttenbrenner. The exact cause of his death is still a matter of debate, with various theories that include alcoholic cirrhosis, syphilis, infectious hepatitis, lead poisoning, sarcoidosis, and Whipple's disease. In 2008, Austrian pathologist Christian Reiter asserted that Beethoven's doctor, Andreas Wawruch, accidentally killed him by administering lead acetate as a treatment for fluid retention.

Different sources mention different people who made Beethoven's death mask. One source states that his death mask was made by Austrian painter, Joseph Dannhauer. However, another states that there is a debate about when the death mask was taken, and that in 1888 Carl Danhauser wrote in a report that the mask was made by Johann Josef Watteroth, a Viennese sculptor. Despite the different sources, it is clear that a death mask of Beethoven was made after his death, although there is much discrepancy as to where it is housed today.

Felix Mendelssohn:

Fig 58

Jakob Ludwig Felix Mendelssohn Bartholdy, known as Felix Mendelssohn, was a celebrated German composer, pianist, conductor, and teacher, widely considered one of the most significant figures of the early Romantic period [73]. Born on February 3, 1809, in Hamburg, Mendelssohn was the grandson of the philosopher Moses Mendelssohn. He was born to Jewish parents, Abraham and Lea Salomon Mendelssohn, from whom he took his first piano lessons. Though the Mendelssohn family was proud of their ancestry, they considered it desirable in accordance with 19th-century liberal ideas to mark their emancipation from the ghetto by adopting a new surname, Bartholdy.

Mendelssohn's musical career began at a young age, and he quickly gained recognition as a prodigious talent. He composed his first published works at the age of 13 and went on to create a large body of works throughout his life, including symphonies, concertos, oratorios, and chamber music. He was also a gifted pianist and conductor and played a significant role in reviving the music of Johann Sebastian Bach.

Mendelssohn suffered from poor health in the final years of his life, probably aggravated by nervous problems and overwork. A final tour of England left him exhausted and ill, and the death of his sister, Fanny, on May 14, 1847, caused him further distress. Less than six months later, on November 4, 1847, aged 38, Mendelssohn died in Leipzig after a series of strokes. Although he had been generally meticulous in the management of his affairs, he died intestate. Mendelssohn's funeral was held at the Paulinerkirche, Leipzig, and he was buried at the Dreifaltigkeitsfriedhof I in Berlin-Kreuzberg.

Mendelssohn's death mask was created by sculptor Gustav Blaeser, which is now in the collection of the Berlin State Library. The museum also has a plaster cast of Mendelssohn's hand, which was made at the same time as the death mask.

Franz Schubert:

Fig 59

Born on January 31, 1797, in Himmelpfortgrund, near Vienna, Franz Schubert grew up in a musical family. He learned violin from his father, who was a schoolteacher, and piano from his brother. Schubert joined the precursor of the Vienna Boys Choir in 1808, where he made such quick progress that Antonio Salier, an influential composer and teacher, became Schubert's mentor and guide, overseeing his training for six years [74].

Schubert's compositions during this time showed great promise, but his career did not take off until he left school and began to earn money as a teacher and composer. Schubert is best known for his Lieder, a type of German song, and is considered one of the greatest composers of the Romantic era. In 1821, Schubert's 20 most popular songs were published with great success, and he wrote the three-act opera *Alfonso und Estrella*.

Despite his first awareness of the disease (possibly syphilis) that would kill him, his amazing production continued in 1822, with the

Unfinished Symphony and the *Wanderer Fantasy*. He was often ill during his last five years but continued his production of music, including the song cycles "The Miller's Beautiful Daughter" and "Winter Journey," the last three piano sonatas, and the "Great Symphony."

Schubert's illness progressed rapidly in his final months, leaving him bedridden and unable to compose. During this time, Schubert's brother Ferdinand and his friend Franz von Schober visited him frequently. Schubert's died on November 19, 1828, at the age of 31 in Vienna. A death mask was made on or after 3 pm on the day of his death. Although, a photograph of it exists on Wiki Media Commons, its maker and current whereabouts are unknown.

Richard Wagner:

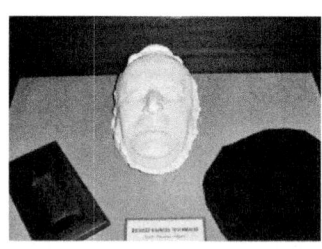

Fig 60

Richard Wagner was a German composer, theatre director, conductor, and polemicist who revolutionized Western music with his operas and music. He was born on May 22, 1813, in Leipzig, Germany, and was the youngest of nine children [75]. Wagner's early years were influenced by his artistic and theatrical background, with several of his elder sisters becoming opera singers or actresses. He was an impulsive and self-willed child who was a negligent scholar at the Kreuzschule, Dresden, and the Nicholaischule, Leipzig. However, he frequented concerts, which helped him develop his musical talent.

Wagner's life was not without controversy. It was characterized by political exile, turbulent love affairs, poverty, and repeated flight from his creditors. His controversial writings on music, drama, and politics have attracted extensive comment, particularly since the late 20th century, where they express anti-Semitic views. Wagner's music was played at the Dachau concentration camp to "re-educate" the prisoners.

Wagner's later years were spent in Venice, Italy, where he passed away on February 13, 1883, at the age of 69, from a heart attack. There is a legend that the attack was prompted by an argument with his wife, Cosima, but it has been debunked. His body was shipped back to Bayreuth, Germany, by gondola and train, where he was buried.

Wagner's death mask was made by the sculptor Gustav Kietz in Venice, Italy, shortly after his death. Although, another source says it was made by sculptor Augusto Benvenuti. The mask is now on display in the Richard Wagner Museum in

Bayreuth, Germany. It is an eerie reminder of the composer's life and legacy.

Franz Liszt:

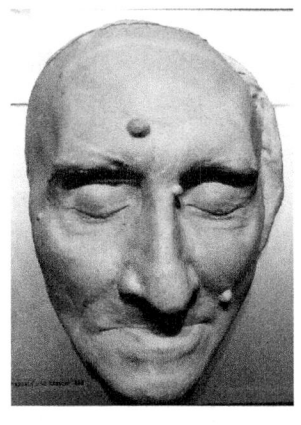

Fig 61

Franz Liszt was a renowned Hungarian composer, pianist, and conductor of the 19th century. Born on October 22, 1811 in Doborján, Hungary (which is now Raiding, Austria), he was the only child of Adam and Anna Liszt [76]. He started playing the piano at the age of six, and by the age of nine, he was already performing in public. At 11, he was accepted to the Vienna Conservatory where he studied composition and piano under the guidance of Carl Czerny and Antonio Salieri.

Despite his success as a musician, Liszt faced personal struggles throughout his life. In 1826, his father passed away, which deeply affected him. He fell in love with one of his piano pupils in 1828, but her father forbade the relationship, causing Liszt to become severely ill. In fact, his obituary was published in a Paris newspaper as he was considered close to death. After his illness, he underwent a long period of recovery.

His career took off in 1831 when he moved to Paris and became a piano virtuoso, performing concerts across Europe. He was known for his flamboyant stage presence and revolutionary performance style. In addition to his career as a performer, Liszt was also a prolific composer. He is considered one of the most influential composers of the 19th century, and his works include symphonic poems, piano concertos, and chamber music. By the time of his death, he had written more than 700 compositions.

Liszt continued to perform and compose into his later years, but his health began to deteriorate. He suffered a stroke in 1881, which left him partially paralyzed, and he died five years later on July 31, 1886, in Bayreuth, Germany. After his death, a death mask was made of his face and is on display at the Liszt Museum in Budapest, Hungary. The museum also has a collection of Liszt's personal belongings, including his piano, manuscripts, and letters.

Johann Strauss II:

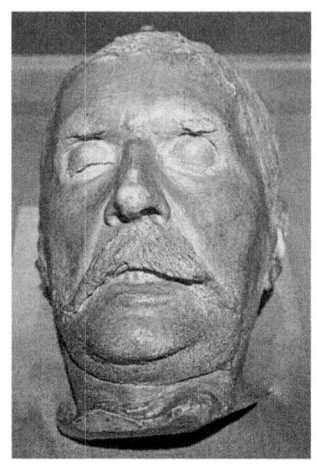

Fig 62

Johann Strauss II, also known as the "Waltz King," was an Austrian composer of light music, particularly dance music and operettas, as well as a violinist. He was born on October 25, 1825, in Vienna, Austria, to composer Johann Strauss I. His father wished him to follow a non-musical profession, so he started his career as a bank clerk. However, he studied the violin and started his career as a musician at a young age, initially playing in his father's orchestra and eventually taking over the leadership of the ensemble after his father's retirement [77].

Strauss II became known for his rhythmic verve and charming melodic design in his works, which included not only waltzes but also galops, polkas, quadrilles, and other dances. In 1872, he conducted concerts in New York City and Boston. Strauss's most famous single composition is *An der schönen blauen Donau* (The Blue Danube).

Strauss II married three times and remained productive until his final days. He was working on a ballet, *Cinderella*, when he fell ill with a respiratory infection that progressed to pneumonia. He passed away on June 3, 1899, in Vienna at the age of 73. At the time of his death, a death mask was made of his face, but it is unclear as to where it is today. One source does indicate that it is on display at the Vienna Museum.

Pyotr Ilyich Tchaikovsky:

Fig 63

Born on April 25, 1840, in Votkinsk, Tchaikovsky was a Russian composer known for his orchestral music, operas, and ballets [78]. He showed a talent for music at a young age. His mother died of cholera when he was just 14 years old. His father was a mining engineer and had hoped that his son would follow in his footsteps. However, Tchaikovsky had a passion for music and began studying piano at the age of five. He went on to attend the Saint Petersburg Conservatory, where he studied under Anton Rubinstein.

Tchaikovsky's music was well-received during his lifetime, and he is considered one of the most popular Russian composers of all time. Some of his most famous works include *Swan Lake*, *The Nutcracker*, and *Romeo and Juliet*. Tchaikovsky's compositions were met with both critical acclaim and controversy. Some of his works, such as the ballet *Swan Lake*, were initially poorly received but went on to become classics. Others, such as his opera *The Queen of Spades*, were criticized for their unconventional harmonies and lack of adherence to traditional musical forms.

Despite his success as a composer, Tchaikovsky struggled with personal problems throughout his life. He was a deeply emotional person who experienced bouts of depression and anxiety, and his homosexuality was a source of great personal turmoil in a society that was deeply hostile to same-sex relationships.

On November 6, 1893, just nine days after the premiere of his Sixth Symphony *The Pathétique*, Tchaikovsky died in Saint Petersburg at the age of 53. The official cause of death was reported to be cholera, which he most likely contracted through drinking contaminated water. The death mask of Pyotr Ilyich Tchaikovsky, created shortly after his death, can be found in the Collection of State Central M. Glinka Museum of Music in Moscow, Russia.

Wolfgang Amadeus Mozart:

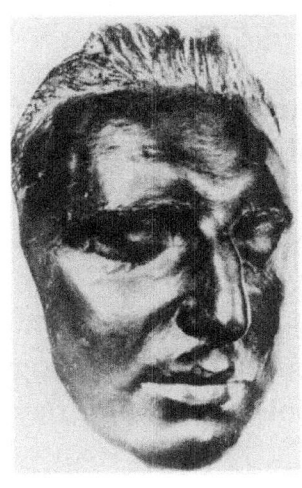

Fig 64

Wolfgang Amadeus Mozart was an Austrian composer born on January 27, 1756, in Salzburg, Austria. He was baptized as Johannes Chrysostomus Wolfgangus Theophilus Mozart and is widely recognized as one of the greatest composers in the history of Western music. Mozart showed prodigious musical talent from an early age and composed his first piece of music at the age of five. He traveled extensively throughout Europe and became a celebrated composer, pianist, and conductor in his time.

Mozart's life was characterized by financial struggles, despite his success as a pianist and composer. By the mid-1780s, his extravagant lifestyle was beginning to take its toll, and he fell into serious debt [79]. Despite this, he continued to compose some of his most well-known works, including operas such as *The Marriage of Figaro* and *Don Giovanni*. Between 1790 and 1791, now in his mid-thirties, Mozart went through a period of great music productivity and personal healing. Some of his most admired works --*The Magic*

Flute, *The Final Piano Concerto in B-flat*, *The Clarinet Concerto in A major*, and *The Unfinished Requiem* to name a few.

On December 5, 1791, Mozart died at the age of 35 in his home in Vienna, Austria. The cause of Mozart's death is uncertain, due to the limits of postmortem diagnosis. Officially, the record lists the cause as severe miliary fever, referring to a skin rash that looks like millet seeds. Since then, many hypotheses have circulated regarding Mozart's death, including poisoning, kidney failure, and rheumatic fever.

There are different accounts of who made Mozart's death mask. One source suggests that Count Joseph Deym von Stritetz made a plaster cast of Mozart's face upon his death and subsequently exhibited the death mask in his gallery. Another source mentions that the death mask is kept at Mozart's old house, which is now a museum called Mozart Haus in Vienna, Austria. However, it is known that the death mask was created by Joseph Lange, a friend of Mozart's, and was used to create a bust of the composer. The mask is now housed in the Mozarteum Foundation in Salzburg, Austria.

Frederic Chopin:

Fig 65

Frédéric Chopin was a renowned Polish-French composer and pianist of the Romantic era. He was born on March 1, 1810, in Żelazowa Wola, near Warsaw, Poland. Chopin's father was a Frenchman who had lived in Poland for many years, and his mother was Polish. Chopin's musical talent was evident from a young age, and he began performing publicly at the age of eight. He studied music in Warsaw and later in Vienna, where he made his performance debut in 1829. Chopin's success in Vienna led to a tour of Europe.

In 1830, Chopin left Poland for Paris, where he quickly established himself as a prominent pianist and composer in the city's music scene [80]. He composed many pieces during his time in Paris, including preludes, nocturnes, and waltzes. However, his health began to decline in the mid-1840s.

In February 1848, a revolution broke out in Paris, which left Chopin broken in spirit and depressed. In an attempt to escape the turmoil in Paris, Chopin accepted an invitation to visit England and Scotland. He was received warmly in London, where he performed at several fashionable parties and gave lessons. The trip was exhausting for Chopin, and he returned to Paris in early 1849, where his health continued to decline.

Chopin died in Paris on October 17, 1849, at the age of 39. The exact cause of his death is still unknown, but it is believed to have been related to his chronic lung disease. His death mask was made by Jean-Baptiste Clésinger, a French sculptor who was a friend of Chopin's. Clésinger made the mask in Paris, shortly after Chopin's death. The death mask is now in the collection of the Musée de la Vie Romantique in Paris. The museum is dedicated to the Romantic era in art and literature, and it has a collection of objects related to Chopin and other Romantic artists.

Josef Leopold Zvonar:

Fig 66

Josef Leopold Zvonar was a Czech composer, pedagogue, music critic, and writer born on June 25, 1824, in Horice na Sumave, Bohemia (now the Czech Republic) [81]. He is considered one of the most important figures in Czech music history, and his work helped to shape the country's national identity.

He studied at the organ school in Prague with Pitsch and worked as an assistant teacher and organist there. He was briefly the school's director. In 1860, he became the director of Žofín Academy, a woman's music school. Zvonar composed overtures, chamber music, cantatas, an opera entitled *Zaboj*, a requiem, and piano works. His music is characterized by a strong sense of melody and a unique blend of Czech and Germanic musical traditions. However, he is best remembered as an educator; he was the author of *The First History of Organology* and *The Art of Teaching*.

Zvonar's life was cut short when he died on November 23, 1865 at age 41, in Prague from tuberculosis. He was buried in the Cemetery at Vysehrad. His death mask was used to create a bust, which is now housed in the Czech Museum of Music in Prague. The museum also holds several of his original manuscripts.

Artists & Sculptors

Josef Moroder Lusenberg:

Fig 67

Josef Moroder-Lusenberg was a prominent painter and sculptor from the Grodenthal in South Tyrol, now known as Val Gardena in Italy. He was born on May 28, 1846, in Urtijei, and lost his father when he was eight years old. He was apprenticed in a wood-carving studio under Franz Prinoth, an academic sculptor educated in the Munich Academy. In his twenties, Josef started his own studio, and examples of his early activity as a sculptor are the wooden statues of the twelve apostles in the parish church of Urtijei.

Lusenberg's artistic style was deeply influenced by the South Tyrolean tradition of woodcarving, and he became renowned for his realistic sculptures, which often depicted scenes from everyday life [82]. He was also a member of the Munich School, which was a group of artists who studied at the Academy of Fine Arts in Munich. He became well known for his paintings and sculptures, and his most famous work is the wooden sculpture of the *Christ on the Cross* in the parish church of Ortisei.

His first wife, Annamaria Sanoner, died after giving birth to their fourth child in 1874. He subsequently married Felizitas Unterplatzer, who gave birth to eleven other children. Josef Moroder-Lusenberg died on February 16, 1939, in Urtijei, at the age of 92. A death mask was created after his death, and it is now on display in the Museum Gherdeina in Urtijei.

Benjamin Robert Hayden:

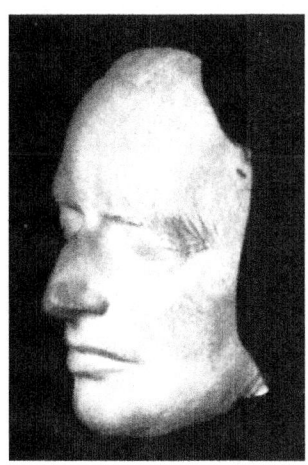
Fig 68

Benjamin Robert Hayden was an English historical painter and writer, born on January 25, 1786, in Plymouth, Devon, England [83]. He was the son of a Plymouth bookseller and went to London to attend the Royal Academy schools. Hayden specialized in grand historical pictures, although he also painted a few contemporary subjects and portraits. His commercial success was damaged by his often tactless dealings with patrons, and by the enormous scale on which he preferred to work.

Haydon's life was marked by personal and financial difficulties. He was imprisoned for debt in 1823 and 1826, and he struggled to support his family with his art. Despite these challenges, Haydon continued to produce paintings and write, and he left instructions for an account of his life to be published after his death.

Haydon's life came to a tragic end on June 22, 1846, when he committed suicide by shooting himself in the head. Hayden's stormy career, down to 1821, is recorded in his autobiography, which with a selection from his journals covering the rest of his life, was published in 1853. The complete text of his Diary was published in 1960–63. Hayden's acquaintance among literary people was extensive, and intimate glimpses of them are given in his autobiography. He was a friend of the poets William Wordsworth, Samuel Taylor Coleridge, and John Keats, and he painted portraits of all three. He also painted portraits of the philosopher Jeremy Bentham and the scientist Michael Faraday.

There is a source that says that Hayden's death mask was made by the sculptor William Behnes shortly after his death. Although, there is no verification from other sources that William Behnes indeed made the mask. The death mask of Benjamin Robert Hayden is now held in the collection of the National Portrait Gallery in London.

Sir Thomas Lawrence:

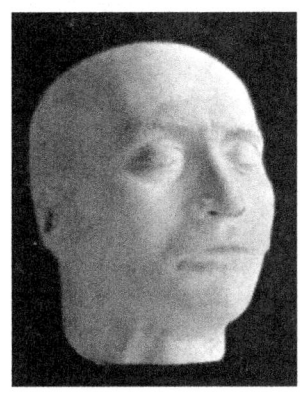

Fig 69

Sir Thomas Lawrence was an English portrait painter who gained popularity during the late 18th and early 19th centuries [84]. Lawrence was born on April 13, 1769, in Bristol, England, to an innkeeper who owned the Black Bear at Devizes. His father's profession exposed him to people from different walks of life, which ignited his passion for drawing. At the age of ten he began to draw portraits of his family and friends.

At the age of 18, he moved to London and gained attention from the art world with his painting of Queen Charlotte. He became the most fashionable English portrait painter of his time and painted many notable personalities, including King George IV, Queen Charlotte, and the Duke of Wellington. Lawrence's polished and flattering style became the pattern of society portraiture to the present day.

Despite his fame, Lawrence had a turbulent personal life. He was plagued by financial difficulties throughout his life. He was a compulsive spender and often found himself in debt. He never married, but he had many romantic relationships that often ended in disappointment. Lawrence's health deteriorated in his later years, and he suffered from a series of strokes. On January 7, 1830, he died in his home at Russell Square, London, at the age of 60.

A death mask was made by Richard James Lane, a British artist, in the days following Lawrence's death. It has been on display in various collections, including the British Museum, the Victoria, Albert Museum, and The Cleveland Museum of Art. It is a testament to Lawrence's enduring legacy as one of the greatest portrait painters of his time.

J. M. W. Turner:

Joseph Mallord William Turner was an English Romantic landscape painter whose works were distinguished by their expressionistic portrayal of light, color, and atmosphere [85]. Turner was born on April 23, 1775, in Covent Garden, London, England, to a wigmaker and barber who

Fig 70

supported the family through his wife's struggles with mental illness. As a child, Turner was sent to live with an uncle in rural England, where he began his artistic career. At age 10, he attended school in Brentford, Middlesex, before returning to London to study at the Royal Academy of Arts.

Turner's early works were realistic, but over time, he developed a more fluid and poetic style that is now regarded as a predecessor to Impressionism. In 1793, the Royal Society of Arts awarded the 17-year-old Turner the "Great Silver Pallet" for landscape drawing. Turner soon earned a steady income through a variety of artistic endeavors, including selling designs to engravers, coloring sketches, and providing private lessons.

Turner's private life was secretive, unsociable, and somewhat eccentric. He never married but had a long-term affair with Sarah Danby, a widow who probably bore him two children. Turner's mother became hopelessly ill in 1800 and was committed to a mental hospital. His father came to live with him and worked as his studio assistant for 30 years. His father's death in 1829 had a profound effect on him, and thereafter he was subject to bouts of depression.

Turner died on December 19, 1851, at the age of 76, in Cheyne Walk, Chelsea, London. The cause of his death was listed as "bronchitis and other lung-related diseases." Turner's death mask is held at the Tate Gallery in London. The mask is attributed to the Pre-Raphaelite sculptor Thomas Woolner, who was a great admirer and collector of Turner's works. The mask portrays Turner's skin as tissue-paper thin, his eyes hollowed, nose pinched, and mouth a shrunken and toothless cavity.

Dante Gabriel Rossetti:

Fig 71

Dante Gabriel Rossetti was a celebrated English painter and poet who was born in London on May 12, 1828 [86]. He was the most prominent member of the Rossetti family and was one of the founders of the Pre-Raphaelite Brotherhood. The group sought to revive the art of the early Italian Renaissance, before the time of Raphael, and to create works that were more truthful to nature.

Rossetti's paintings often featured medieval or Arthurian themes, and he was known for his use of vivid colors and intricate details. Rossetti's paintings were extremely influential in European art and often depicted women in close-up, dense compositions that featured floral elements.

Rossetti's personal life was often tumultuous. He had several affairs, including one with his model and muse, Elizabeth Siddal, whom he later married. Siddal died of a laudanum overdose in 1862, and Rossetti was devastated. He buried a manuscript of his poems with her, which he later exhumed and published as *The House of Life*.

Towards the end of his life, Rossetti's health began to deteriorate. He suffered from obesity, addiction, bad eyesight, and paranoia, which was worsened by the consumption of chloral (a sedative). He suffered two breakdowns in 1877 and 1879. He also suffered from Bright's disease (a kidney condition) and was housebound for several years. He died on April 9, 1882, at the age of 53, in Birchington-on-Sea, Kent, England.

After Rossetti's death, his brother William had a death mask made of him. The mask was created by Domenico Brucciani, an Italian sculptor who was known for his work in the field of death masks. The mask was in the possession of W. M. Rossetti up until his death. It is unknown as to its whereabouts currently.

Wilhelm von Kaulback:

Fig 72

Wilhelm von Kaulbach was a German painter, muralist, and illustrator who was born on October 15, 1804, in Arolsen bei Kassel, Hesse-Kassel, Germany [87]. He was associated with the German Romantic movement and is considered one of the most important German history painters of the 19th century. Kaulbach studied under Peter von Cornelius at the Dusseldorf Academy from 1822. When Cornelius became director of the academy in Munich in 1824, he brought Kaulbach to Munich. Kaulbach succeeded Cornelius in 1843 as the academy's director—a position he held for 25 years.

In his work, he presented an idealized vision of history, which fed a nationalistic spirit and appealed to contemporary taste. A more ironic edge is sometimes discernible in his illustrations, as seen in his drawings for *Reynard the Fox* (1846–47), although his illustrations for the works of Johann Wolfgang von Goethe, Friedrich von Schiller, and William Shakespeare are traditional and somewhat conservative.

Kaulbach's popularity declined, and he had to witness, not without inquietude, the rise of an opposing party of naturalism and realism. He is perhaps best known for his monumental frescoes in the stairway of the New Museum in Berlin, which depict the history of art from ancient Egypt to the 19th century. Other notable works include *The Destruction of Jerusalem*, *The Battle of the Huns* (which inspired a symphonic poem by Franz Liszt), *The Crusaders at the Gates of Jerusalem*, and *The Age of the Reformation*. *The Destruction of Jerusalem* was a copy of an earlier oil painting, much admired by Friedrich Wilhelm I of Prussia, which was by then already in the collection of Ludwig I of Bavaria.

Wilhelm von Kaulbach died on April 7, 1874, in Munich, Germany, at the age of 69. He is buried in the Alter Sudfriedhof in Munich. It is not clear who created the death mask or where it is currently located. However, it is likely that the death mask is held in a museum or private collection in Germany.

Antonio Canova:

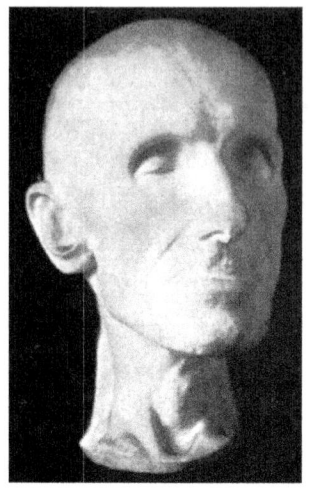
Fig 73

Antonio Canova was an Italian sculptor who was born in Possagno, a small village in the Republic of Venice on November 1, 1757 [88]. He was the son of Pietro Canova, a stonecutter and a sculptor, who introduced him to the world of art at a young age. Canova showed a natural talent for sculpture and was apprenticed to his father at the age of nine.

Canova moved to Venice in 1775 and began working for the sculptor Giuseppe Bernardi, also known as Torretto. In 1779, he moved to Rome, where he studied classical art and drew from the nude. He also made plaster casts from live models. Canova was in Rome in 1779 and 1780, where he met the leading artists of the period, including the Scottish painter-dealer Gavin Hamilton, who directed Canova's studies toward a more profound understanding of the antique. Canova visited Naples and the ancient ruins of Pompeii and Herculaneum, where he studied the art of the ancient Greeks and Romans.

Canova's reputation as a sculptor grew, and he was eventually invited to work in Vienna, where he became the official court sculptor to Emperor Francis II. He remained in Vienna for nearly 20 years, during which time he created many of his most famous works, including the monument to Archduchess Maria Christina and the statue of Theseus and the Minotaur.

Canova died in Venice on October 13, 1822, at the age of 64. His death was widely mourned throughout Europe, and he was buried in the Temple of Possagno, which he had designed himself. It is not clear who made Canova's death mask. Some sources say it was made by the sculptor Bartolomeo Ferrari while others say it was made by his assistant, Adamo Tadolini. The mask is now housed in the Gipsoteca Canoviana museum in Possagno, Italy, which was founded by Canova himself. The museum contains many of Canova's works, as well as his personal effects.

James John Audubon:

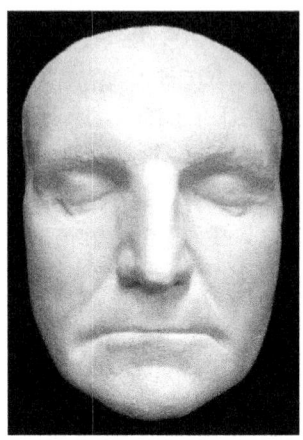

Fig 74

John James Audubon was an ornithologist, artist, and naturalist who became particularly well-known for his drawings and paintings of North American birds. He was born on April 26, 1785, in Les Cayes, Saint-Domingue, West Indies (now Haiti) [89]. After trying and failing in several different types of business ventures, he concentrated on drawing and studying birds.

In 1803, when Audubon was 18, war broke out between France and England. To keep him from being conscripted into the Emperor Napoleon's army, his father sent him to his estate in Mill Grove, Pennsylvania. Changing his name to John James Audubon en route, he wholeheartedly embraced the American wilderness and its avian inhabitants. There he conducted his first scientific studies.

After trying and failing in several different types of business ventures, he concentrated on drawing and studying birds and began traveling extensively to pursue his passion. He became progressively more intimate with the natural environment and dedicated to documenting it.

By 1824, Audubon had grown intent on finding a publisher for his work but was unable to generate any serious interest in the United States. Two years later, he set sail for the United Kingdom, where he hoped to at least be able to find engravers skilled enough to properly reproduce his work. The decision immediately proved a good one. He exhibited his work at the Royal Academy, where it was seen by a prominent group of ornithologists and art critics. He was soon offered a subscription to produce *The Birds of America*, and his future was assured.

Audubon spent most of his last decade in New York, having succumbed to various illnesses, and died there on January 27, 1851. He is buried in Trinity Church Cemetery in Washington Heights, New York City. Audubon's death mask was made two days after his death by John Henry Brown, an artist and sculptor, and is now part of the collection of the New-York Historical Society.

Jacques-Louis David:

Fig 75

Jacques-Louis David was born on August 30, 1748, in Paris, France, into a prosperous family. His father was a small dealer in textiles who was killed in a duel when David was nine years old. His mother left him with his well-off architect uncles, who saw to it that he received an excellent education at the Collège des Quatre-Nations.

David was a significant influence in French art, especially academic Salon painting. He had many pupils, making him the strongest influence in French art of the early 19th century. As an artist during the years of Napoleon's dictatorship, David was frequently busy with revolutionary propaganda. He had commemorative medals struck, set up festivals, and designed costumes and scenery for plays.

David's work was closely associated with the French Revolution, and he was a member of the National Convention during the Reign of Terror. He supported the revolution and created propaganda art for the revolutionary cause, including his famous painting *The Death of Marat* in 1793. However, he later fell out of favor with the new government and was imprisoned briefly during the Reign of Terror. After the fall of Robespierre in 1794, David was released from prison and continued to work as a painter, creating portraits of Napoleon Bonaparte and other political figures [90].

David died on December 29, 1825, in Brussels, Belgium, where he had earlier fled after the fall of Napoleon. He was buried in the cemetery of Sainte-Gudule in Brussels, but his remains were later exhumed and reinterred in the Père Lachaise Cemetery in Paris in 1848.

The death mask of Jacques-Louis David is on display in the Musée du Louvre in Paris, France. The mask is part of the collection of the museum's Department of Sculptures. David was known to have been interested in death masks and had a collection of them himself.

Vojtech Preissig:

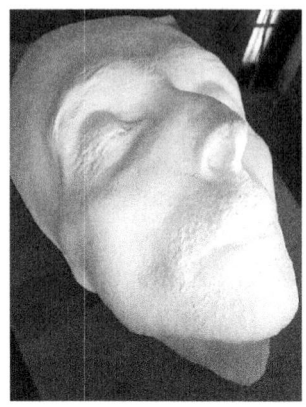

Fig 76

Vojtech Preissig was a Czech typographer, printmaker, designer, illustrator, painter, and teacher. He was born on July 31, 1873, in Světec, northern Bohemia, and his father was a mining engineer. In 1884, he moved to Prague, where he studied at the School of Applied Industrial Art from 1892 to 1896, then at the School of Decorative Architecture from 1897 to 1898. He returned to Prague in 1899 and worked as a freelance artist and designer. In 1903, he became a teacher at the School of Applied Industrial Art in Prague, where he taught until 1910. He then moved to the United States and worked as a freelance artist and designer in New York City.

Pressing's work was highly influential in the development of modern graphic design. He was a pioneer in the use of typography as a design element, and his work was characterized by bold, geometric shapes and strong, simple lines.

Vojtech Preissig was arrested in 1940 for his involvement in resistance activities after returning to Czechoslovakia [91]. He was then imprisoned and transported to the concentration camp in Dachau. He arrived there on January 29, 1944, and tragically died there on June 11, 1944, at the age of 70. The circumstances of his death are not clear, but it is believed that he was executed by the Nazis.

It is also not clear who made the death mask of Preissig. One source believes it was Frantisek Muzika, a Czech sculptor, while another indicates that it was Frantisek Muzika, a French artist. Both were at Dachau at the time. The mask is currently on display in the Museum of Dachau memorial site at Dachau.

Egon Schiele:

Fig 77

Egon Schiele was an Austrian expressionist artist who was born on June 12, 1890, in Tulln, near Vienna. He is most famous for his expressionistic and often sexually explicit depictions of the human body [92]. As a student at the Vienna Academy of Fine Arts from 1907 to 1909, Schiele was heavily influenced by the Jugendstil movement, also known as the German Art Nouveau. Schiele's work often featured distorted and elongated figures that conveyed intense emotional and psychological states.

Schiele's life was marked by controversy, particularly due to his alleged employment of the town's teenage girls as models. He and his lover, Wally Neuzil, were driven out of several towns by residents who disapproved of their lifestyle. Schiele's work was also controversial, and he was arrested in 1912 for obscenity. Despite this, Schiele continued to produce art that was both provocative and innovative.

Schiele's death was tragic and sudden. His wife, Edith Harms, died on October 28, 1918, during the Spanish flu pandemic. Schiele himself died just three days later, on October 31, 1918, also from the flu. He was only 28 years old at the time of his death.

After Schiele's death, a death mask was made of his face. The whereabouts of the death mask is not clear, but it is believed to be in the possession of the Leopold Museum in Vienna. The museum has a large collection of Schiele's work, including his famous painting *Death and the Maiden*. The painting memorializes the end of Schiele's affair with Neuzil, conveying this separation as the death of true love.

Hiram Powers:

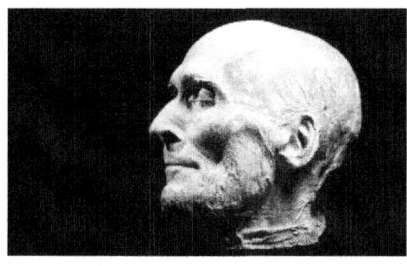

Fig 78

Hiram Powers was an American sculptor born on July 29, 1805, in Woodstock, Vermont. He was the son of a farmer and was raised in a rural environment. At the age of 17, he moved to Cincinnati, Ohio, where he worked as a coach maker's apprentice. He later became interested in art and began to study sculpture. In 1837, he moved to Italy, where he spent the rest of his life.

Powers was known for his neoclassical style and his ability to capture the human form in marble. His most famous work, *The Greek Slave* [93], was a sculpture of a woman in chains that was exhibited in London and New York in the mid-19th century. The sculpture was a commentary on the issue of slavery in the United States and was widely popular.

Powers continued to create several other sculptures, including portrait busts of famous individuals such as President Andrew Jackson. He also established a studio in Florence, Italy, where he continued to work and gain fame for his neoclassical style of sculpting.

Powers died on June 27, 1873, in Florence, Italy, at the age of 67. He was buried in the Protestant Cemetery in Florence. A death mask of his face was created by Joel Tanner Hart, another American sculptor living in Italy. The death mask of Hiram Powers is now in the collection of the Smithsonian American Art Museum in Washington, D.C.

Political Leaders & Activists

Napoleon Bonaparte:

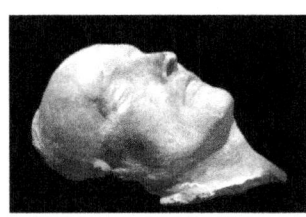

Fig 79

Napoleon was born on August 15, 1769, in Ajaccio, Corsica, and was the fourth child of Carlo Buonaparte, a lawyer, and his wife, Letizia Ramolino. He became a French general and first consul in 1799-1804, and then an emperor of the French from 1804-1814/15. He fought in the French Revolutionary Wars and led France through a series of wars known as the Napoleonic Wars.

Napoleon was educated at three schools, including the military academy in Paris, where he was trained as an artillery officer. He quickly rose through the ranks of the French military and became a general at the age of 24. Napoleon's military campaigns were marked by his strategic genius and his ability to inspire his troops.

He conquered much of Europe and established a vast empire that included France, Italy, Spain, and parts of Germany and Poland. He also introduced a number of reforms that modernized France, including the Napoleonic Code, which established a uniform legal system throughout the country. Despite his many successes, Napoleon's empire began to crumble in the early 19th century. He suffered a number of military defeats, including the disastrous Russian campaign of 1812, and was eventually exiled to the island of Elba.

He escaped from Elba in 1815 and briefly regained power in France before being defeated at the Battle of Waterloo and was exiled again, this time to the remote island of Saint Helena in the South Atlantic. Napoleon spent the last six years of his life on Saint Helena, where he was closely monitored by the British authorities. He died on May 5, 1821, at the age of 51, and was buried on the island on May 9 in the presence of French and English witnesses [94]. It is said that Napoleon dressed and presented himself as the grand Emperor he once was throughout his life and while in exile. On his deathbed, however, he was reduced to a mere human.

During that time, it was customary to cast a death mask of a great leader who had recently died. A mixture of wax or plaster was placed over Napoleon's face and removed after the form had hardened. From this impression, subsequent copies were cast. Much mystery and controversy surrounds the whereabouts of the original mold and casts. Napoleon's original death mask was created on May 7, 1821, a day and a half after the former emperor died.

The whereabouts of the original cast molds are unknown. However, there are other death masks of Napoleon that are still in existence, including two plaster masks kept at the Maison Bonaparte in Ajaccio, Corsica and a bronze mask that was presented at the Cabildo in New Orleans and is now on display at the Louisiana State Museum.

Robert Emmet:

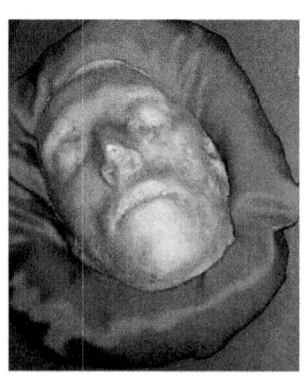

Fig 80

Robert Emmet was an Irish nationalist and rebel who played a crucial role in the movement for Irish independence. Born in Dublin on March 4, 1778, Emmet was the youngest son of Dr. Robert Emmet, a state physician, and his wife Elizabeth Mason. Despite his father's desire for him to become a lawyer, Emmet developed a strong interest in politics and became involved in the nationalist movement at a young age.

Emmet became involved in the United Irishmen, a revolutionary group that sought to overthrow British rule in Ireland. In 1803, he led an unsuccessful rebellion against the British government. He was captured, tried for treason, and sentenced to death. On September 20, 1803, Emmet was executed in Thomas Street in front of St. Catherine's. He was hanged and then beheaded once dead. His body was buried in an unmarked grave, which has never been traced. However, his legacy lived on, and he became a symbol of Irish nationalism.

Emmet's death mask was made by his friend James Petrie at the jail where the body was left [95]. The death mask is now in the collection of the National Museum of Ireland and is considered to be one of the museum's most significant artifacts. It is believed to be the only surviving death mask of an Irish rebel leader and is a powerful symbol of Ireland's struggle for independence.

Joseph Stalin:

Fig 81

Joseph Stalin was born on December 18, 1878, in Gori, Georgia, Russian Empire. He was the second leader of the Soviet Union. He joined the Bolsheviks in 1903 and rose through the ranks of the Communist Party in the early 1920s. After Lenin's death in 1924, Stalin became the leader of the Communist Party and consolidated his power through a series of purges that eliminated his political opponents [96].

In 1928, Stalin abandoned Lenin's quasi-capitalist New Economic Policy in favor of headlong state-organized industrialization under a succession of five-year plans. The Soviet Union was transformed from a peasant society into an industrial powerhouse under Stalin's leadership, but at a great human cost. Millions of people were forced into labor camps or executed as part of Stalin's purges and policies of collectivization. Despite this, he is credited leading the Soviet Union into the nuclear age.

Stalin's health began to deteriorate towards the end of World War II. He had atherosclerosis as a result of heavy smoking, a mild stroke around the time of the Victory Parade in May 1945, and a severe heart attack in October 1945. His condition continued to deteriorate, and he died at 9:50 p.m. on March 5, 1953, at his Kuntsevo Dacha, after suffering a stroke. The last three days of Stalin's life have been described in detail, first in the official Soviet announcements in Pravda, and then in a complete English translation which followed shortly thereafter in the Current Digest of the Soviet Press.

After his death, Stalin's body was embalmed and placed on public display in Moscow's Red Square. His death mask, a plaster cast of his face made after his death, was also created, which is currently in the Gori Stalin Museum.

Thomas Paine:

Thomas Paine was an English-born American Founding Father, political activist, philosopher, political theorist, and revolutionary. He was born on January 29, 1737, in Thetford, Norfolk, England, to a Quaker father and an Anglican mother. His formal education was meager, just enough to enable him to master reading, writing, and

Fig 82

arithmetic. At 13, he began work with his father as a corset maker and then tried various other occupations unsuccessfully. He had two brief marriages and was unsuccessful or unhappy in every job he tried. In 1774, he met Benjamin Franklin in London, who advised him to immigrate to America, which he did.

He quickly became involved in the American independence movement and began writing pamphlets and essays advocating for independence from British rule. His most famous work, *Common Sense*, published in 1776, argued for the necessity of independence and helped to rally support for the cause. He continued to write influential works throughout the war, including *The American Crisis* series [97].

In his later years, Paine lived in poverty and obscurity. Despite his contributions to American independence and democracy, Paine was not well-liked by many Americans. He was criticized for his radical views and his criticism of organized religion. Derided by the public and abandoned by his friends, he died on June 8, 1809, at the age of 72 in New York City. According to his obituary in the New York Citizen, "He had lived long, did some good, and much harm." His funeral was attended by only a handful of people, including his doctor and a few former slaves. He was buried in an unmarked grave in New Rochelle, New York.

After his death, Paine's reputation began to improve, and he was recognized as an important figure in American history. In 1819, William Cobbett, a British political writer and friend of Paine's, obtained Paine's death mask and some of his bones. Cobbett intended to give Paine a heroic reburial on his native soil, but this never came to pass. The bones were still among Cobbett's effects when he died over a decade later. In 1839, the American sculptor John Wesley Jarvis created a bust of Paine based on the death mask. The bust is now in the collection of the New-York Historical Society.

Aaron Burr:

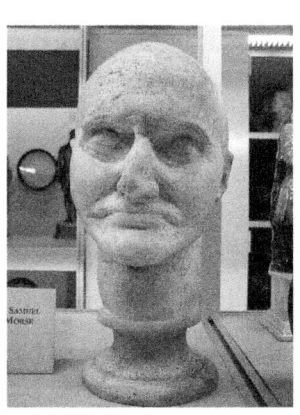

Fig 83

Aaron Burr was a prominent American politician and lawyer who served as the third Vice President of the United States from 1801 to 1805. He was born on February 6, 1756, in Newark, New Jersey. Burr's parents died when he was young, and he was raised by his uncle. He graduated from the College of New Jersey (now Princeton University) at the age of 16 and went on to study law.

During the Revolutionary War, Burr served as an officer in the Continental Army, and he was commended for his bravery. After the war, Burr started a legal practice in New York City, and he was soon elected to the New York State Assembly. In 1791, he was elected to the U.S. Senate, where he became known for his skills as an orator and debater. In the 1800 presidential election, Burr was the running mate of Thomas Jefferson. The election resulted in an electoral vote tie between Jefferson and Burr, and the decision went to the House of Representatives. After 36 ballots, Jefferson was elected president, and Burr became vice president.

Burr's political career took a turn for the worse after he killed his political rival, Alexander Hamilton, in a duel in 1804. Hamilton had opposed Burr's candidacy for governor of New York, and Burr challenged him to a duel. Hamilton was mortally wounded, and Burr fled to Philadelphia. He was later charged with murder in both New York and New Jersey but was never convicted. After his acquittal, he fled to Europe, where he lived for four years before returning to New York.

Burr's later years were marked by personal tragedy. He lost his beloved daughter Theodosia Burr Alston when the ship she was on disappeared off the coast of North Carolina in

1813. He fell ill during one of his business trips, but instead of staying at home and gaining strength, he continued to work and travel, which eventually led to his death on September 14, 1836.

It is not known who made Burr's death mask, but according to a story on boweryboyshistory.com [98], when Burr died in his room, a stranger appeared at the door and made a plaster death mask of the Vice President. The mask is now part of the collections of the New-York Historical Society, and it is occasionally displayed in exhibitions.

Daniel O'Connell:

Fig 84

Daniel O'Connell, also known as "The Liberator", was a lawyer and the first great 19th-century Irish nationalist leader. He was born on August 6, 1775, near Cahirciveen, County Kerry, Ireland, in Genoa, Kingdom of Sardinia (now Italy). O'Connell was a prominent figure in the Catholic Emancipation movement, which aimed to end discrimination against Catholics in Ireland. He was also a proponent of Irish independence and founded the Repeal Association in 1840, which sought to repeal the Act of Union that had merged Ireland with Great Britain.

O'Connell's journey began when he was forced to leave the Roman Catholic college at Douai, France, due to the outbreak of the French Revolution. He then moved to London to study law and became a lawyer. His dedication to his cause and leadership skills quickly propelled him to become the first great Irish nationalist leader of the 19th century [99].

O'Connell's rise to prominence began in the 1820s, when he organized a series of mass meetings in Ireland to demand Catholic Emancipation. He was elected to the British Parliament in 1828, but was initially prevented from taking his seat because he refused to take the oath of allegiance to the British monarch, which conflicted with his Catholic faith. However, he was eventually able to take his seat in 1829, after the Catholic Emancipation Act was passed.

Despite his success, O'Connell faced opposition from both the British government and some Irish nationalists. He was criticized for his moderate approach to Irish independence, which some saw as insufficiently radical. He was also accused of being too willing to work with the British government, which many Irish nationalists saw as an enemy of Irish independence.

O'Connell's health began to decline in the 1840s, and he suffered a series of strokes that left him partially paralyzed. He died on May 15, 1847, in Genoa, Italy, at the age of 71. His body was brought back to Ireland and buried at Glasnevin cemetery in Dublin.

A death mask of Daniel O'Connell was created within an hour of his passing. There is some speculation that it was made by Italian sculptor Giovanni Maria Benzoni at the request of O'Connell's son, but that is unverified. What is known for sure is that the mask had been in the custodianship of the Dunraven family for over 160 years. It was presented to the Office of Public Works by the Countess of Dunraven in August 2019.

William McKinley:

Fig 85

William McKinley was the 25th President of the United States, serving from 1897 until his assassination in 1901. He was born on January 29, 1843, in Niles, Ohio, to a family of modest means. He briefly attended Allegheny College, and was teaching in a country school when the Civil War broke out. Enlisting as a private in the Union Army, he was mustered out at the end of the war as a brevet major of volunteers. He studied law, opened an office in Canton, Ohio, and married Ida Saxton, daughter of a local banker.

McKinley rose to prominence as a lawyer and politician, serving in the U.S. House of Representatives from 1877 to 1891 before being elected Governor of Ohio in 1891 and 1893. He was elected President in 1896.

Under McKinley's leadership, the United States went to war against Spain in 1898 and acquired a global empire, which included Puerto Rico, Guam, and the Philippines [100]. McKinley was re-elected in 1900, campaigning against William Jennings Bryan. His second term, which had begun auspiciously, came to a tragic end in September 1901. On September 6, he was shot twice by Leon Czolgosz, an anarchist, at the Pan-American Exposition in Buffalo, New York. McKinley died on September 14 of gangrene caused by the wounds. He was the third American president to be assassinated, following Abraham Lincoln in 1865 and James A. Garfield in 1881.

Following McKinley's passing, a death mask was created to preserve his likeness. McKinley's death mask is currently held in the collection of the Buffalo History Museum in Buffalo, New York, near the site of his assassination. The mask is one of several artifacts related to McKinley's life and death that are on display at the museum. The museum also has a comprehensive collection of primary source materials on the McKinley assassination, including photographs, newspaper articles, and personal accounts.

Theodore Roosevelt:

Fig 86

Theodore Roosevelt, also known as Teddy Roosevelt, was the 26th President of the United States, serving from 1901 to 1909. He was born on October 27, 1858, in New York City. He started his political career as a Republican leader and was elected to the New York legislature in 1882. In 1901, Roosevelt became president after William McKinley's assassination, making him the youngest person ever to hold the office at the age of 42 [101]. During his presidency, Roosevelt focused on expanding the power of the federal government to regulate business and promote social justice, earning him the nickname of the "Trust Buster."

Roosevelt was also a writer, naturalist, and soldier. One of his most significant accomplishments was the establishment of national parks and forests, which he believed were essential to preserve America's natural beauty and resources for future generations. He also won the Nobel Peace Prize in 1906 for his efforts in ending the Russo-Japanese War.

In 1884, he left politics after the deaths of both his mother and his wife on the same day. After his wife and mother's death, Roosevelt spent much of the next two years on his ranch in the Badlands of Dakota Territory. There he mastered his sorrow as he lived in the saddle, driving cattle, hunting big game, and even once capturing an outlaw.

Roosevelt died in his sleep on January 6, 1919, at the age of 60, due to a pulmonary embolism at his family home in Oyster Bay, New York. A death mask was made of his face by the American sculptor James Earle Fraser shortly after his death. Fraser was a sculptor who had previously created a bust of Roosevelt. The mask is now housed at the Museum of Natural History in New York City.

Vladimir Lenin:

Fig 87

Vladimir Lenin was born on April 10, 1870, in Simbirsk, Russia [102]. He was intellectually gifted and physically strong, and he displayed a voracious passion for learning from an early age. He graduated from high school ranking first in his class and distinguished himself in Latin and Greek. Lenin was destined for the life of a classical scholar, but he was influenced by two blows that led him to take the path of revolution. First, his father was threatened shortly before his untimely death with arrest and exile for his revolutionary activities. Second, his older brother was executed in 1887 for plotting to assassinate Tsar Alexander III.

Lenin's political career began in the late 1890s when he joined the Russian Social Democratic Labor Party. His revolutionary activities began in 1895 when he joined the Marxist movement. He was soon arrested and exiled to Siberia, but escaped to Western Europe in 1900. Lenin spent the next 17 years in exile, organizing the Bolshevik Party and writing political tracts. He returned to Russia in 1917 and led the Bolshevik

Revolution, which overthrew the Provisional Government and established the world's first socialist state.

Lenin's health began to decline in 1922, and he suffered a series of strokes that left him partially paralyzed. He died on January 21, 1924, at the age of 53, in Gorki, near Moscow. The official cause of death was recorded as an incurable disease of the blood vessels. Lenin was given a state funeral and then buried in a specially erected mausoleum on Red Square in Moscow.

His death mask is made of bronze and was created by the sculptor Sergey Merkurov. It is now on display in the State Historical Museum in Moscow. The death mask is a haunting reminder of Lenin's legacy and the impact he had on the world. It is a symbol of the Soviet Union and the communist movement, and it continues to inspire and provoke debate to this day.

Lorenzo De' Medici:

Fig 88

Lorenzo de' Medici, also known as "Lorenzo the Magnificent," was born in Florence, Italy on January 1, 1449 [103]. He was a patron of the arts and letters, and his court was a gathering place for artists, poets, and philosophers. He supported the work of Michelangelo, Botticelli, and Leonardo da Vinci, among others. He also founded the Platonic Academy, a group of scholars who studied the works of Plato and other ancient philosophers. Lorenzo himself was a poet and wrote several works, including a collection of sonnets.

Lorenzo ruled Florence with his younger brother, Giuliano, from 1469 to 1478, and after Giuliano's assassination, Lorenzo continued to rule the city-state until his own death. In declining health for some three years, Lorenzo died on April 9, 1492, at the age of 43. While on his deathbed, he was visited by Girolamo Savonarola, a Dominican friar who had been preaching against the corruption of the church and the Medici family. Savonarola reportedly asked Lorenzo to repent of his sins, but Lorenzo refused, saying that he had never done anything wrong. After Lorenzo's death, Savonarola became a powerful figure in Florence and led a campaign of moral reform that included the burning of books, art, and other items deemed immoral or pagan.

Lorenzo Di' Medici's original mask is owned by the Società Colombaria in Florence and is currently on deposit at the Museo degli Argenti in Palazzo Pitti, Florence. The mask is a cast of Lorenzo's actual face and is a haunting likeness that suggests the forceful intelligence behind his power. The mask is not handsome, but it is full of dignity as to compel respect. There are also modern after casts of the mask that are available for viewing. One such after cast is owned by the National Gallery of Art in Washington, D.C., and is on display in the West Building, Ground Floor, Italian Renaissance galleries.

Eva Peron:

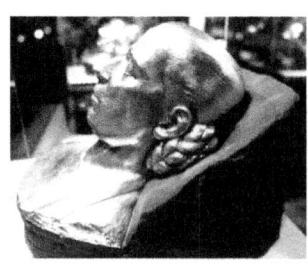

Fig 89

Eva Perón was born on May 7, 1919, in Los Toldos, Argentina. Her family struggled financially, and the situation worsened when her father died when she was just six years old. A few years later, the family moved to Junín, Argentina. At the age of 15, Eva traveled to Buenos Aires to pursue an acting career, eventually landing radio parts [104]. It was during this time that she met Juan Perón, who was then serving as the Secretary of Labor and Social Welfare. The two married in 1945, and Eva quickly became involved in her husband's political career, working to improve the lives of the poor and marginalized in Argentine society.

Eva's political career was not without controversy. She was criticized by the military and bourgeoisie for her populist policies and her growing influence over her husband's administration. Her declining health also became a concern, and in 1951, when she was diagnosed with cervical cancer, she obtained the nomination for vice president. However, the army forced her to withdraw her candidacy.

In the months leading up to her death, she grew noticeably ill, and her last public appearance was in June 1952, when she accepted the title "Spiritual Leader of the Nation." Eva Perón's death at the age of 33 on June 26, 1952 was a tragic event that left a deep impact on Argentine society. She was given a state funeral, and her body was embalmed and put on display for several years. Her death mask, a plaster cast of her face, was also made and became a popular item among her supporters. The death mask was used to create a bronze statue of Eva, which was unveiled in Buenos Aires in 1955. The statue became a symbol of Eva's legacy and was later moved to the Eva Perón Museum in Buenos Aires.

However, Eva's death mask may have contributed to a darker side. In 2015, a neuroscientist named Dr. Daniel Nijensohn claimed that Eva had undergone a lobotomy shortly before her death. According to Nijensohn's theory, the lobotomy was performed by a surgeon who was not qualified to do so and was done without Eva's consent. The operation was allegedly carried out to control Eva's pain and anxiety, but it left her in a vegetative state and hastened her death. Nijensohn's theory has been controversial, and many experts have disputed his claims. However, the story of Eva's death mask remains a fascinating and tragic part of Argentine history.

Politicians & Statesmen

John Philpot Curran:

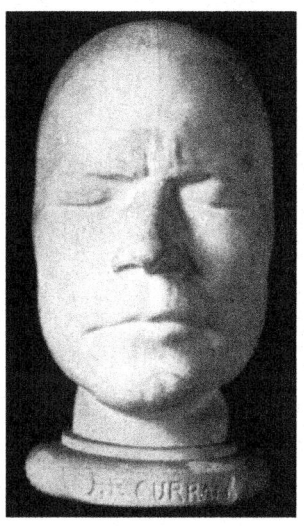

Fig 90

John Philpot Curran was an Irish politician, lawyer, and renowned orator who passionately defended civil and political liberty during his time. He was born on July 24, 1750, in Newmarket, County Cork, Ireland. Curran was educated in grammar and the classics by Nathaniel Boyse, the rector of Newmarket. Although handicapped by small stature and a speech impediment, he soon became celebrated for his quick wit and courage in defending apparently hopeless cases.

Curran's notable moment in the public eye came in 1780 when he stood up for a Catholic priest who had been horsewhipped by an Anglo-Irish Lord. At the time, he was the only lawyer in his circuit willing to take on the case, which earned him popular support and recognition [105]. Throughout his career, he consistently championed the cause of Irish rights and liberties, leaving a lasting impact on the legal and political landscape of Ireland.

Curran's life was marked by personal turmoil. His favorite daughter Gertrude fell to her death in 1792 and he buried her in the grounds of the Priory where he would spend hours watching her grave from his window. In 1794 he discovered that his wife had become pregnant by a lover and he refused to stand in the general election later that year.

He passed away on October 14, 1817, in Brompton, Middlesex, England. Although it is unknown who made John Philpot Curran's death mask, there is at least one sources indicating that it is held at Trinity College Dublin, and is part of their collection of historical artifacts.

Lord Palmerston:

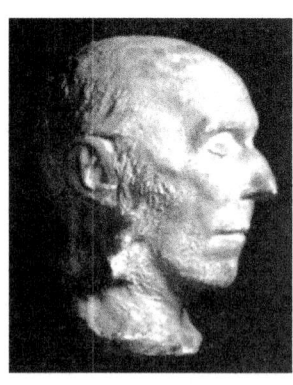

Fig 91

Lord Palmerston, born Henry John Temple, was an English Whig-Liberal politician who served as Prime Minister of the United Kingdom twice, from 1855 to 1858 and from 1859 to 1865. He was born on October 20, 1784, in Broadlands, Hampshire, England. Palmerston was studious at Cambridge, and the young junior minister was thought a bit of a recluse.

He had a long and distinguished career in politics, beginning in 1807 when he entered Parliament as a member of the Tory party. Over the years, he switched affiliations and became associated with the Whig-Liberal party. One of his notable roles was serving as British Foreign Secretary from 1830 to 1834 [106].

Palmerston was a master at controlling public opinion by stimulating British nationalism. Although Queen Victoria and most of the political leadership distrusted him, he received and sustained the favor of the press and the populace, from whom he received the affectionate nickname "Pam." Palmerston's personal security was essential to get to the very top of British politics. Lady Palmerston was his best advisor and most trusted amanuensis.

During his tenure as Prime Minister, Lord Palmerston focused on various domestic and foreign policy issues. He championed liberalism and democracy, advocating for parliamentary reform, religious freedom, and international trade. He also played a key role in shaping Britain's foreign relations, particularly during significant events such as the Crimean War and the American Civil War.

When Palmerston died on October 18, 1865 at Brocket Hall in Hertfordshire, many people thought that an era had definitely ended, and that parliamentary and Irish reform would be set back. His last words were, "Die, my dear doctor? That's the last thing I shall do!" While some scandalous rumors surrounded his death, it is important to note that these were not substantiated.

A death mask of Lord Palmerston was taken immediately after death at Brockton Hall by a Mr. Jackson. Only one cast was ever made and upon this was based the head upon the statue of Palmerston by Mr. Jackson, now in Westminster Abbey. The existence and/or whereabouts of the original casting remain unknown.

Benjamin Disraeli:

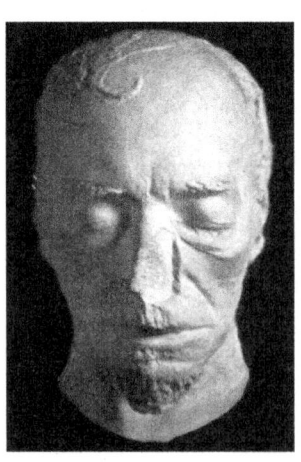

Fig 92

Known as Benjamin Disraeli, earl of Beaconsfield, he was a prominent British statesman and novelist. He was born on December 21, 1804, in London, England. Disraeli served as Prime Minister of the United Kingdom on two occasions playing a signifycant role in shaping British politics and the Conservative Party [107].

Disraeli's political career began in the mid-19th century when he was elected to the House of Commons. He served as Chancellor of the Exchequer and Leader of the House of Commons before becoming Prime Minister. Throughout his political career, Disraeli implemented a twofold policy of Tory democracy, which aimed to reconcile the interests of the aristocracy and the working class. He is known for his skillful oratory and his ability to connect with the masses, as well as for his reformist and imperialistic vision. Disraeli's policies included social reforms, such as the Public Health Act of 1875, as well as expansionist initiatives, including the acquisition of shares in the Suez Canal.

Disraeli was also a prolific writer and published several novels throughout his career. His first novel, *Vivian Grey*, was published in 1826-27 and sold well but caused much offense in influential circles when the authorship was discovered. His last completed novel, *Endymion*, was published shortly before his death.

On April 19, 1881, Benjamin Disraeli passed away in London, marking the end of a remarkable political career. In honor of Disraeli, an annual day called Primrose Day is held every year on April 19, the anniversary of his death. Primroses were his favorite flowers, and Queen Victoria even sent a bunch of primroses to adorn Disraeli's grave at his funeral.

A death mask was taken six hours after Disraeli's death. It is currently held by the British Museum, but it is not available for public viewing. It seems that there is some uncertainty regarding the authenticity of the mask because it lacks the famous wart that Disraeli was known to have. The mask was taken off public display in 1954.

Daniel Webster:

Fig 93

Daniel Webster was an influential American lawyer, orator, and politician who played a significant role in the early history of the United States. Born on January 18, 1782, in Salisbury, New Hampshire, he grew up in a family of farmers. His father served in the local militia during the War for Independence, and Daniel was one of ten children [108].

Daniel Webster's political career began in 1813 when he was elected to the U.S. House of Representatives. He served two non-consecutive terms in the House, from 1813 to 1817 and again from 1823 to 1827.

Webster was known for his eloquent speeches and his strong support for a strong federal government and the Union during the Civil War. He was also a strong advocate for the rights of Native Americans and worked to protect their interests during his time in Congress. In addition to his political career, Webster was also a successful lawyer and argued many important cases before the Supreme Court.

In 1827, Webster was elected to the U.S. Senate, where he would serve for a total of 20 years, in two separate periods. He was a prominent figure in the Senate, known for his impassioned speeches on various issues, including the protective tariffs and nullification crisis. His most famous speech, known as the "The Most Famous Senate Speech," was delivered on January 26, 1830, and emphasized the importance of preserving the Union.

In addition to his work in Congress, Webster also held the position of U.S. Secretary of State. He served as the 14th Secretary of State under Presidents William Henry Harrison from 1841 to 1843, and then again as the 19th Secretary of State under Millard Fillmore from 1850 to 1852. As Secretary of State, Webster was involved in various diplomatic negotiations and played a crucial role in expanding U.S. trade with other nations.

Webster died on October 24, 1852, at his home in Marshfield, Massachusetts. His death was caused by injuries he sustained after falling out of a carriage. After his death, a death mask was created to preserve his likeness. It is now held in the collection of the New York Public Library.

Jean Paul Marat:

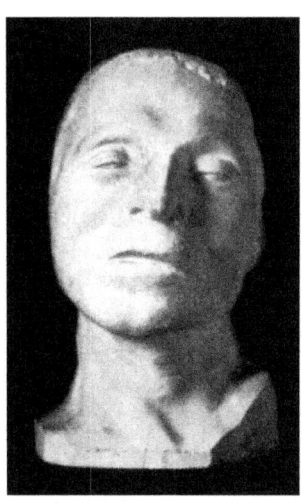

Fig 94

Jean-Paul Marat was a prominent figure in the French Revolution and a leader of the radical Montagnard faction [109]. He was born on May 24, 1743, in Boudry, near Neuchâtel, Switzerland, and later became a well-known doctor in London during the 1770s. Marat left home as a teenager and travelled to Paris, where he undertook studies in medicine and set up practice as a doctor. He wrote articles and books on science and medicine, including one on the treatment of scrofula, which earned him a prize from the Academy of Sciences.

Marat became involved in politics during the French Revolution and used his newspaper *L'Ami du Peuple* (Friend of the People) to promote his radical views. He was known for his fiery rhetoric and his calls for violence against those he saw as enemies of the revolution. Marat was also a member of the National Convention, which governed France during the revolution.

Marat was assassinated in his bath by Charlotte Corday, a young Girondin conservative who had come to Paris to kill him. Initially denied entrance to Marat's apartment she changed her clothing and went to a hairdresser, hoping to appear more alluring. Corday arrived at Jean-Paul Marat's apartment at around 7 pm on July 13th, 1793. This time she was allowed to enter by offering information about Girondinist plotting in her native Normandy. Marat was desperately unwell and, according to some sources, already close to death. Riddled with eczema and weeping skin lesions, he took frequent medicinal baths to relieve his skin infection, and Marat received her while in the bath. Corday, however, had ulterior motives and fatally stabbed him. The assassination of Marat became a significant event during the French Revolution, with varying interpretations and consequences.

It is unclear as to who made Marat's death mask, but one source indicates that it is on display at the Musée Carnavalet in Paris. It is a haunting reminder of the violence that characterized the French Revolution and the impact that Marat had on this tumultuous period in history.

Henry George:

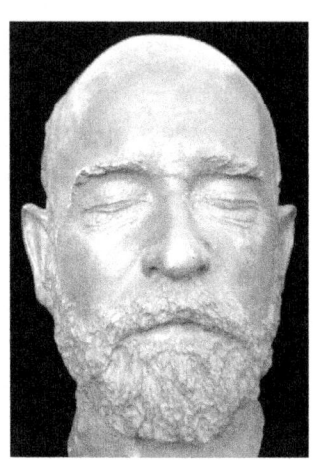

Fig 95

Henry George was an American political economist, journalist, and social reformer. He was known for his work on the single tax, which proposed that the state should tax away all economic rent, the income from the use of bare land but not from any improvements made on the land. His seminal work on this subject, *Progress and Poverty*, was published in 1879.

George was a popular writer in 19th-century America and his ideas sparked several reform movements of the Progressive Era. He inspired the economic philosophy known as Georgism, which believes that people should own the value they produce themselves, but that the economic value derived from land should be shared equally by society.

Henry George's passionate advocacy for land reform and his economic theories resonated with many during his time. His work inspired social protests and earned him a reputation as one of the most compelling speakers for social change [110]. However, despite his influence, George did not hold political office and focused primarily on his writing and public speaking.

George died on October 29, 1897, at the age of 58, in New York City, New York. He suffered two strokes during his life, and he was in the middle of a mayoral campaign at the time of his death. After his death, his admirers created a death mask of his face, which was donated to Princeton University by his wife, Annie Corsina Fox George, in 1937.

Count Cavour:

Fig 96

Count Camillo Benso di Cavour, born on August 10, 1810, in Turin, Piedmont, was an influential Italian statesman and a key figure in the Risorgimento, the movement for Italian unification in the 19th century [111]. He played a crucial role in the political and diplomatic landscape of

Italy, eventually leading to the unification of the country under the House of Savoy. Cavour's life was marked by his astute diplomacy, exploitation of international rivalries, and strategic alliances that contributed to the formation of a unified Italian nation.

Cavour was educated at home and later attended the University of Turin. After completing his studies, he entered the civil service, where he quickly rose through the ranks due to his intelligence and strong work ethic. In 1848, he was elected to the Piedmontese parliament, where he quickly became a leader of the liberal opposition.

In 1852, he was appointed as the Minister of Agriculture, Commerce, and Navigation in the Piedmontese government. He quickly implemented a series of reforms that helped to modernize the Piedmontese economy and increase its competitiveness. In 1858, Cavour became the Prime Minister of Piedmont-Sardinia, and he began to work towards the unification of Italy. He formed an alliance with Napoleon III of France and used this alliance to defeat Austria in the Second Italian War of Independence in 1859. This war resulted in the annexation of Lombardy by Piedmont-Sardinia.

Soon after, Cavour's health began to deteriorate rapidly, and he died on June 6, 1861, in Turin, Italy. He was immediately considered one of the protagonists of the political unification of Italy. After his death, Italy would gain Venice in 1866 in the course of the Austro-Prussian War and Rome in 1870, with the help of the French.

Cavour's death mask was made immediately after his death. It is currently on display at the Central Museum of the Risorgimento in Rome. The museum is dedicated to preserving and showcasing artifacts related to the Italian Risorgimento, including significant figures such as Cavour.

Charles Sumner:

Fig 97

Born on January 6, 1811, in Boston, Massachusetts, Charles Sumner was raised in a middle-class family [112]. He graduated from Harvard College in 1830, and after briefly studying law in the Harvard Law School, he embarked on a grand tour of Europe, immersing himself in European culture, history, and political philosophies.

Upon his return to the United States, Sumner became a prominent lawyer and legal scholar. However, his true passion lay in politics and the abolitionist movement. In 1851, he was elected to the United States Senate, representing Massachusetts. Sumner quickly gained notoriety for his speeches against the spread of slavery and the injustices inflicted upon African Americans.

On May 22, 1856, Sumner delivered a speech titled "The Crime against Kansas," in which he criticized the pro-slavery forces in the Kansas Territory. Two days later, Representative Preston Brooks of South Carolina confronted Sumner as he sat writing at his desk in the almost empty Senate chamber. Brooks beat Sumner with a cane until he was unconscious. Sumner's traumatic injuries kept him absent through most of the next four years as a congressman, but he was nevertheless reelected to a second term and continued to oppose any compromise with the south in the years leading up to the Civil War.

On March 11, 1874, Charles Sumner passed away at the age of 63, marking the end of a remarkable political career. Sumner's death reverberated throughout the nation, and he was mourned by many who recognized the profound impact he had made on American society.

Sumner's death mask was made shortly after his death by Clark Mills, a sculptor who was known for his work on the statue of Andrew Jackson in Lafayette Square in Washington, D.C. The location of the mask is unclear, but at least one source indicates that it is now part of the collection of the National Museum of American History.

Maximillian Robespierre:

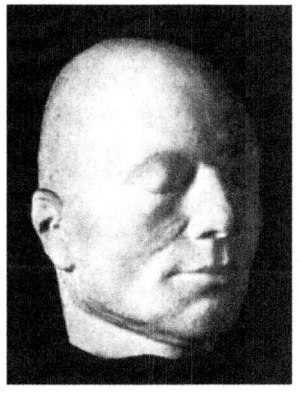

Fig 98

Maximilien de Robespierre was a French revolutionary leader who played a significant role in the French Revolution. He was born on May 6, 1758, in Arras, France, to a lawyer father and a mother who died when he was six years old. After his mother's death, his father left home, and Maximilien, along with his brother and sisters, was raised by his maternal grandparents. From 1765 he attended the college of the Oratorians at Arras, and in 1769 he was awarded a scholarship to the Lycée Louis-le-Grand in Paris. He graduated with distinction and took up the study of law.

Robespierre's political career gained momentum when he was elected a deputy of the Estates-General in 1789, and he soon became a staunch advocate for political change and the rights of the people [113]. Robespierre became a successful lawyer in Arras from 1781 to 1789. He was elected to the National Assembly in 1789, where he became notorious as an outspoken radical in favor of individual rights. He became a leading member of the Montagnards in the National Convention. After calling for the death of Louis XVI, he led the Jacobins and the Committee of Public Safety (1793) in establishing the Reign of Terror during which, as virtual dictator of France, he had former friends such as Georges Danton executed.

Despite earlier support from the people of Paris, who called him "the Incorruptible," he lost his dominating authority and was overthrown and guillotined in the Thermidorian Reaction on July 28, 1794. Robespierre's legacy remains controversial to this day. Some view him as a monster who had thousands of people killed to maintain power while others see him as a hero and fighter for the people against tyranny.

Robespierre's death mask was made after his execution. The mask is now held at the Musée Carnavalet in Paris.

Religious Leaders, Theologians, & Notables

Martin Luther:

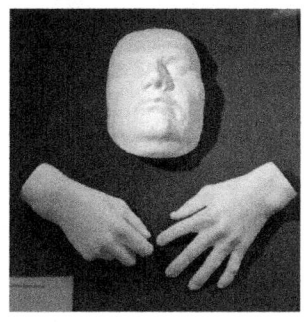

Fig 99

Martin Luther was a German theologian and religious reformer who was the catalyst of the 16th-century Protestant Reformation. He was born on November 10, 1483, in Eisleben. Through his words and actions, Luther precipitated a movement that reformulated certain basic tenets of Christian belief and resulted in the establishment of the Lutheran, Reformed, and Anglican traditions within Christianity.

Luther was a man of deep faith and conviction, and his life was marked by a series of dramatic events that shaped his thinking and his legacy. One of the most famous stories about Luther's life is the story of his "conversion" to the monastic life. According to legend, Luther was caught in a violent thunderstorm near the village of Stotternheim, and he vowed to become a monk if he survived. Although Luther's vow was made under duress, he took it seriously and entered the Augustinian order.

His teachings focused on the doctrine of justification by faith alone, which means that people are saved by their faith in God's grace alone and not by good works. He also translated the Bible into German, making it accessible to more people and helping to spread his ideas.

Martin Luther died at age 62 on February 18, 1546, in Eisleben, the town of his birth. According to a letter he wrote to a friend one month before his death, he was experiencing infirmities of old age and was "old, weary, lazy, worn-out, [and] cold" [114].

A death mask was made of Luther's face (and hands) after his death. The mask was made by pressing a wet plaster mold onto Luther's face, which was then allowed to dry and hardened. The mask would have been used to create a sculpture or painting of Luther's likeness. It is now housed in the Lutherhaus museum in Wittenberg, Germany.

In addition to the death mask, it is also said that Luther's body was exhumed twice. The first time was in 1556, ten years after his death, to move his remains from the local cemetery to the Castle Church in Wittenberg, where he had preached. The second time was in 1830, when his body was exhumed again and his skull was measured to help determine the size of his brain.

Martin Luther King Jr.:

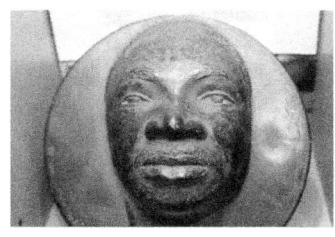
Fig 100

Martin Luther King Jr. was a Baptist minister and social activist who led the civil rights movement in the United States from the mid-1950s until his death by assassination in 1968. He was born Michael King Jr. on January 15, 1929, in Atlanta, Georgia, to a comfortable middle-class family steeped in the tradition of the Southern Black ministry. Both his father and maternal grandfather were Baptist preachers. King was named after Protestant reformer Martin Luther. In 1934, King's father, a respected Atlanta pastor known then by his birth name of Michael King Sr., traveled to Germany with a group of Baptist ministers. While in Germany, he became inspired by the Protestant Reformation leader Martin Luther and changed his own name as well as his son's name to Martin Luther King Jr.

King played a pivotal role in the Montgomery Bus Boycott in 1955. The boycott was sparked by the arrest of Rosa Parks, who refused to give up her bus seat to a white passenger. As a result, the Supreme Court ruled that segregation on public buses was unconstitutional [115].

King continued to lead nonviolent protests against segregation and racism throughout the South. He was instrumental in organizing the March on Washington for Jobs and Freedom in 1963, during which he gave his famous "I Have a Dream" speech in front of the Lincoln Memorial. The march attracted a crowd of over 250,000 people and is considered a turning point in the civil rights movement.

On April 4, 1968, King was assassinated in Memphis, Tennessee, by James Earl Ray. A single shot was fired that caused a fatal wound to the lower right side of his face. SCLC aides rushed to him, and Ralph Abernathy cradled King's head as he lay on the balcony of the Lorraine Motel. King was taken to St. Joseph's Hospital, where he was pronounced dead at 7:05 p.m. His death signaled the seeming end of a period of civil rights progress that he had led and for which his life had become a symbol.

King's death mask is now part of the collection at the National Museum of African American History and Culture in Washington, D.C.

St. Ignatius of Loyola:

St. Ignatius of Loyola, born Iñigo López de Loyola in 1491 in Loyola, Spain, was a Spanish theologian and mystic who became one of the most influential figures in the Roman Catholic Counter-Reformation. He was the youngest of thirteen children and grew up in a family of minor nobility. As a young man, he was known for his love of music and his abundance of reddish hair. He was also a soldier and was badly wounded in battle in 1521, which left him with a lifelong limp.

During his recovery, he had a spiritual conversion that led him to dedicate his life to serving God [116], and founding the Society of Jesus, also known as the Jesuits, in 1534. The Jesuits became known for their missionary work and their commitment to education, which included founding schools and universities. St. Ignatius was also known for his spiritual writings, which include the *Spiritual Exercises*, a guide for people seeking to deepen their relationship with God.

St. Ignatius died on July 31, 1556, in Rome, Italy, at the age of 65. He had been suffering from various illnesses and was thought to be dying as early as 1550. He was buried in the Church of the Gesù in Rome, which was built by the Jesuits in the late 16th century. He was canonized by Pope Gregory XV in 1622 and his feast day is celebrated on July 31.

Ignatius' death mask is particularly interesting because it was made by a famous artist named Alessandro Algardi. Algardi was a sculptor known for his lifelike portraits. The death mask of Ignatius is now kept in the Church of the Gesù in Rome.

Jose Maria Morelos:

Fig 102

Jose Maria Morelos y Pavon was a Mexican Roman Catholic priest, military leader, and politician who played a significant role in Mexico's independence movement in the early 19th century. He was born on September 30, 1765, in Valladolid, Mexico, to a poor "pardo" (Afro-Mexican) family of indigenous and Spanish descent. He worked as a muleteer and cowhand until he began studying for the priesthood at the Colegio de San Nicolas in 1790. After his ordination in 1799, he served as a parish priest in various towns in southern Mexico.

Morelos became involved in the Mexican independence movement in 1810, after the rebel priest Miguel Hidalgo was executed. He assumed leadership of the movement and led several successful campaigns against the Spanish forces. Morelos was an exceptional military commander who was responsible for several key victories against the Spanish, including the capture of Oaxaca, Valladolid, and Acapulco. He was known for his tactical expertise, strategic thinking, and his ability to inspire his troops to fight for their country's independence. However, despite his success, Morelos was captured by the Spanish in 1815 and was subsequently tried and executed for treason on December 22 of that year in San Cristobal [117].

Morelos is considered a national hero of Mexico, and the state of Morelos and city of Morelia are named after him. His remains were transferred to the Independence Column in Mexico City in 1823. Morelos has been portrayed on the 50-peso note since 1997 and on 1-peso coins during the 1940s, 1970s, and 1980s. Morelos' death mask is on display at the National Museum of Anthropology in Monterrey, Mexico.

Pope Pius IX:

Fig 103

Pope Pius IX, born Giovanni Maria Mastai-Ferretti, was the head of the Roman Catholic Church from 1846 to 1878, the longest verified papal reign in history [118]. He was born on May 13, 1792, in Senigallia, Papal States, and died on February 7, 1878, in Rome, Italy, at the age of 85. Pius IX was beatified on September 3, 2000, by Pope John Paul II, and his annual liturgical commemoration is on February 7, the date of his death.

Pius IX's early life was marked by delicate physical constitution but very lively intelligence. He first came into prominence as archbishop of Spoleto from 1827 to 1832, a time of revolutionary disturbance. He was made bishop of the important diocese of Imola in 1832, but it was his election as pope in 1846 that marked the beginning of his most significant role in the Church.

Pius IX's papacy was marked by a number of significant events, including the First Vatican Council, which he convened in 1869, and the promulgation of the doctrine of papal infallibility, which he defined in 1870. He was also responsible for a number of reforms in the Church, including the abolition of the Jewish ghetto in Rome and the establishment of the Pontifical Academy of Sciences.

Pius IX's death was marked by widespread mourning and was seen as the end of an era. His body was embalmed and placed on display for public veneration before being interred in a simple grave and later exhumed, and placed in a crypt of St. Peter's Basilica.

There is some discrepancy regarding who created the death mask of Pope Pius IX. While some sources suggest that the sculptor Enrico De Rossi created the mask without the pope's permission, others suggest that the Italian-born sculptor Costantino Nivola created the mask.

Thomas Chalmers:

Fig 104

Thomas Chalmers was a Scottish minister, professor of theology, and political economist who was born on March 17, 1780, in Anstruther, Fife, Scotland. He was a leader of both the Church of Scotland and the Free Church of Scotland. He received his education at the University of St. Andrews and later studied theology at the University of Edinburgh [119]. He was ordained as a minister of the Church of Scotland in 1803 and quickly became known for his powerful sermons.

Besides being a prominent figure in the Scottish church, his influence extended beyond the church walls. He was a passionate advocate for the poor and believed that the church had a responsibility to address social issues. He was also a vocal opponent of the established church's control over education, arguing that education should be available to all, regardless of their religious background.

Chalmers died on May 31, 1847, at the age of 67. His death was a great loss to the Scottish church and society, and his funeral was attended by thousands of mourners. The death mask of Thomas Chalmers was made by William Brodie, a Scottish sculptor, shortly after his death. Brodie was known for his portraits of prominent Scottish figures, and his death mask of Chalmers was one of his most significant works. The mask is currently held in the collection of the Scottish National Portrait Gallery in Edinburgh.

Harry Edwards:

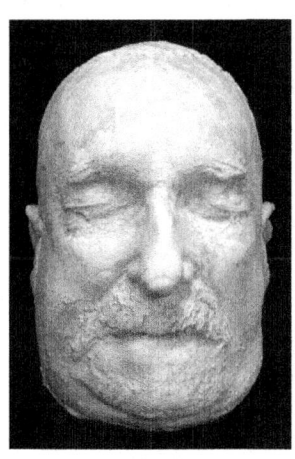

Fig 105

Harry Edwards was a healer, teacher, and author who dedicated nearly 40 years to his career [120]. Born in Islington, London, Edwards was the son of a printer and a dressmaker and grew up as one of nine children. He gained recognition for his spiritual healing abilities, attracting both distinguished individuals and ordinary people who testified to his remarkable talent.

During his lifetime, Edwards was a popular public figure who presented healing in a non-religious, down-to-earth manner. In addition to his work as a healer, Edwards was also an advocate for civil rights and social justice. He was involved in the Olympic Project for Human Rights (OPHR), which aimed to protest against racial segregation in sports.

Edwards treated patients directly at his Healing Sanctuary in Britain or on the platform at public meetings, and also by "absent healing" through correspondence. He worked closely with physicians and believed that spiritual healing power passed through him with the assistance of discarnate spirit helpers. He also claimed to have traveled outside his body to visit distant patients. Edwards authored a number of books and published a monthly magazine *The Spiritual Healer* from his home.

Edwards died on December 7, 1976, at the age of 83. There is no information available about who made his death mask. Although, there is a death mask of Edward's in the Laurence Hutton Collection at Princeton University.

Joseph and Hyrum Smith:

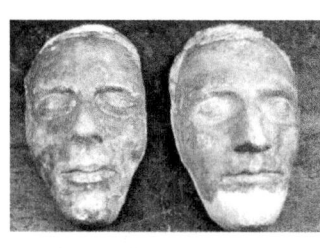

Fig 106

Joseph Smith was the founder and leader of the Latter Day Saint movement, and his brother, Hyrum Smith, was a prominent leader in the church. On June 27, 1844, while awaiting trial in Carthage Jail in Carthage, Illinois, the Smith brothers were killed by a mob. According to historians, the murders were not a spontaneous act by a few personal enemies of the Mormon leaders, but a deliberate political assassination committed or condoned by some of the leading citizens in Hancock County, Illinois [121].

Afterwards, their bodies were taken to Nauvoo, Illinois where they were washed and prepared for burial. The bodies were then photographed, and death masks were made.

The death of Joseph and Hyrum Smith was a tragic event that had a significant impact on the Latter Day Saint movement. Their deaths led to a period of turmoil and uncertainty for the church, but it also galvanized the members and strengthened their resolve to continue the work that Joseph Smith had started.

The events surrounding their deaths are detailed in a timeline created by the Church News in collaboration with the Church History Department. The timeline explains that it is unknown who actually shot Joseph and Hyrum Smith, but Willard Richards and John Taylor made a list of people they recognized in the mob. In October 1844, nine men were indicted for the murders, and in May 1845, only five of those men were tried, but they were all acquitted by a non-Mormon jury.

The death masks of Joseph and Hyrum Smith are significant artifacts in the history of the Latter Day Saint movement. They serve as a reminder of the persecution and violence that the early members of the church faced. The powder horn of a man who participated in the killings of Joseph and Hyrum Smith is also in the possession of the Church History Museum. It is inscribed with the words "Warsaw Regulators, The end of the Polygamist Joseph Smith kilt at Carthage Jail June 27, 1844."

The death masks of Joseph and Hyrum Smith are now in the possession of the Church History Museum in Salt Lake City, Utah.

Criminals

Sacco and Vanzetti:

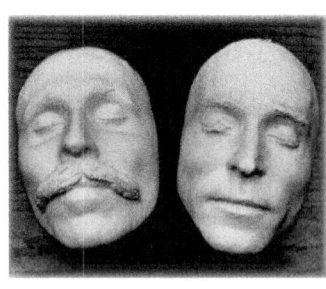

Fig 107

Nicola Sacco and Bartolomeo Vanzetti were Italian immigrants who became symbols of the international left after being wrongly convicted of murder and executed in 1927. The trial and execution of the two men were mired in controversy, and their case remains a topic of debate to this day [122].

Sacco was born in 1891 in Italy, while Vanzetti was born in 1888. Both men immigrated to the United States in the early 1900s, seeking a better life. Sacco worked as a shoemaker, while Vanzetti worked odd jobs, including as a fish peddler and a factory worker. Both men became involved in anarchist activism, advocating for workers' rights and against capitalism.

In April 1920, a payroll clerk and a security guard were shot and killed during a robbery in South Braintree, Massachusetts. Sacco and Vanzetti were arrested and charged with the crime, despite little evidence linking them to the murders. The trial was fraught with bias against the defendants, who were both Italian and anarchists. The judge in the case was openly hostile to the defense, and the jury was made up entirely of white, Protestant men.

Despite a lack of concrete evidence, Sacco and Vanzetti were found guilty and sentenced to death. The case became an international cause célèbre, with protests and rallies held around the world in support of the two men. Despite ongoing appeals and efforts to secure a new trial, Sacco and Vanzetti were executed in the electric chair on August 23, 1927.

There were two sets of death masks made of Sacco and Vanzetti. The first set was made by Dr. Laurence H. Robbins, a physician and amateur sculptor who was allowed to make casts of the faces of Sacco and Vanzetti shortly after their executions. These masks are now housed in the collection of the Historical Society of Massachusetts.

The second set of death masks was made by Edward W. Forbes, who was a director of the Fogg Art Museum at Harvard University and a skilled maker of death masks. Forbes was asked by the Sacco-Vanzetti Defense Committee to make casts of the faces of the two men before their burial, and he did so on August 27, 1927. These masks are now held in the Harvard University Collection of Historical Scientific Instruments.

Ned Kelly:

Fig 108

Ned Kelly, who was born in Beveridge, Victoria sometime between December 1854 and June 1855, was the most famous of the Australian bushrangers (rural outlaws of the 19th century). Kelly's father, John Kelly, was an Irish convict who was transported to Australia for stealing two pigs. Ned Kelly spent close to two weeks in police custody at the age of 14 after assaulting a Chinese pig farmer. In October 1870, he was arrested again for assault. In 1877, Kelly shot and injured a policeman who was trying to arrest his brother, Dan Kelly, for horse theft.

In December 1878, Ned Kelly formed the Kelly Gang with his brother Dan Kelly, Steve Hart, and Joe Byrne. The group became infamous for a string of daring robberies, including the Euroa Bank and the Jerilderie Bank. They were also known for their daring escapes from police custody.

Eventually, the Kelly Gang was brought down by sustained police attack. Ned Kelly was wounded several times and the other gang members were killed. Ned Kelly was tried for murder in Melbourne and found guilty. He was executed by hanging at Melbourne Gaol on November 11, 1880. After his execution, Kelly's body was left suspended for 30 minutes to ensure he was dead.

Soon after he was wheeled to the "dead-house" where several death masks were made, which was customary for executed criminals at the time. They were used for phrenological analysis, to create a record of the deceased, and for public display. Kelly's death masks revealed that his features had not been disfigured, and he had died with a placid expression on his face. One of the masks was displayed at the Wax Museum in Bourke Street owned by Maximilian Kreitmayer.

Despite his criminal activities, Kelly remains a controversial figure in Australian history, with some viewing him as a folk hero who stood up against oppression, while others see him as a cold-blooded killer [123].

Ned Kelly's death masks are on display at various locations. One of the original death masks is on display at the Old Melbourne Gaol, where Kelly was hanged in 1880. Another death mask is on display at the National Portrait Gallery in Australia.

Richard Parker:

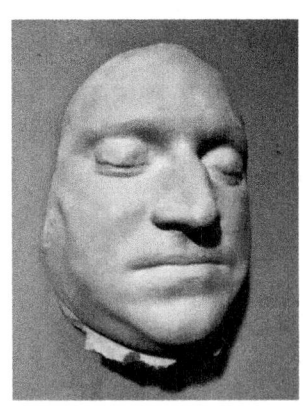

Fig 109

Richard Parker was born on 16 April 1767, and was the son of a well-to-do London merchant [124]. He joined the Royal Navy at the age of 13 serving on various ships before being assigned to the HMS Sandwich, which was widely regarded as one of the worst in terms of its squalid and overcrowded conditions.

Parker played a key role in what is called the "Nore Mutiny of 1797." It was in response to the low pay, poor living conditions, and harsh punishments meted out by the Admiralty. The mutineers formed what was called the "Floating Republic," which was made up of 28 ships, and elected Parker as their leader. However, the mutiny was eventually crushed by the Royal Navy, and Parker was arrested.

Parker's trial was swift, and he was found guilty of treason. He was sentenced to death, and on June 30, 1797, he was hanged on board HMS Sandwich in Portsmouth Harbour. After Parker's execution a death mask was made of his face. The exact details of the making of Parker's death mask are not well-documented, but it is believed that the mask was made by an unknown artist shortly after Parker's execution. Once source mentions that the death mask is displayed at the Royal College of Surgeons in London. Another source mentions that a plaster death mask of Parker was bequeathed to the Royal Naval Museum in Portsmouth.

William Palmer:

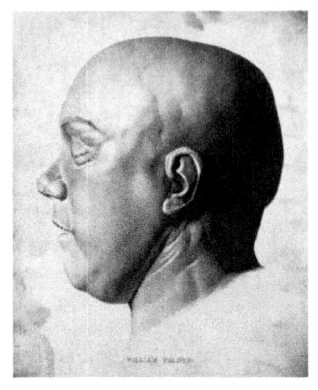

Fig 110

William Palmer, also known as the "Rugeley Poisoner" or the "Prince of Poisoners," was an English doctor who was found guilty of murder in one of the most notorious cases of the 19th century. He was born on August 6, 1824, in Rugeley, Staffordshire, England, the sixth of eight children of Sarah and Joseph Palmer. His father worked as a sawyer and died when William was aged 12, leaving Sarah with a legacy of £70,000. Palmer was educated at a local school and later trained as a doctor in London. He returned to Rugeley in 1847 and married Ann Thornton, with whom he had six children.

Palmer had taken out three life insurance policies on her, totaling £13,000. She died in September 1854, and in January of the following year, Palmer insured his brother Walter for the same amount. Walter died that August [125]. Besides his wife and brother, Palmer was suspected of poisoning several other people, including his mother-in-law. He was also suspected of killing several of his children, as well as a friend, John Parsons Cook. Cook was a wealthy sportsman who had lent Palmer money, and it is believed that Palmer killed him to get out of the debt. Cook died on November 30, 1855, after drinking a glass of brandy that Palmer had given him. Palmer was arrested and charged with murder.

Palmer's trial began on April 14, 1856, and lasted for 12 days. The prosecution presented evidence that Palmer had purchased strychnine, a deadly poison, and had administered it to Cook. The defense argued that Cook had died of natural causes, and that Palmer had no motive to kill him. However, the jury found Palmer guilty, and he was sentenced to death by hanging.

Palmer was executed on June 14, 1856, at Stafford Prison. After his death, a mold of his face was taken to cast a death mask. It is still in existence and can be seen at the National Justice Museum in Nottingham, England. It shows a man with a strong jawline, high cheekbones, and a prominent nose. His eyes are closed, and his mouth is slightly open, giving the impression that he is sleeping.

John Dillinger:

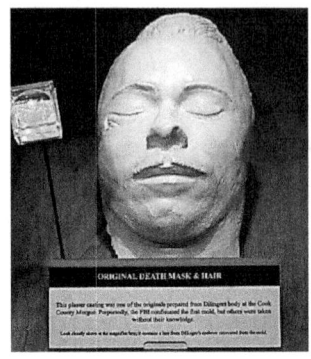

Fig 111

John Herbert Dillinger Jr. was a notorious American bank robber and criminal who was born on June 22, 1903, in Indianapolis, Indiana. He was the youngest of two children and grew up in a middle-class family. Dillinger's criminal career began in 1924 when he was arrested for auto theft. He was sentenced to 10 to 20 years in prison but, he managed to escape from the Indiana State Prison in 1933 using a fake gun to intimidate the guards.

After escaping, Dillinger quickly returned to a life of crime and became one of the most wanted criminals in the United States. He and his gang robbed banks and police arsenals, and they were responsible for the deaths of several police officers. Dillinger became a folk hero to many Americans who were struggling during the Great Depression, and he was known for his daring escapes from jail.

On July 22, 1934, Dillinger was gunned down by FBI agents outside the Biograph Theater in Chicago, Illinois. He had gone to see the movie

Manhattan Melodrama with his girlfriend, Polly Hamilton. When Dillinger left the theater, he was surrounded by FBI agents who shot him three times. He died instantly from a shot that entered the base of his neck, severed his spinal cord, and exited below his right eye [126].

After his death, a plaster death mask was cast of Dillinger's face. The mask was used to create a wax figure of Dillinger that was displayed in the "Crime Doesn't Pay" exhibit at the 1934 World's Fair in Chicago. The mask was created by Dr. Calvin Goddard, a forensic scientist who was involved in the investigation of Dillinger's death. A cast of the death mask is on display at the National Museum of Crime & Punishment, Washington, D.C.

James Bloomfield Rush:

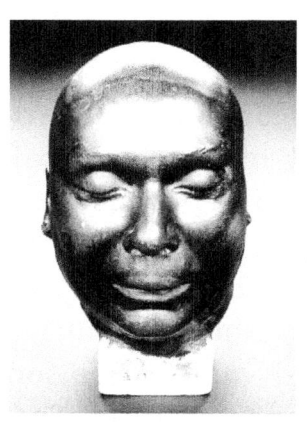

Fig 112

James Bloomfield Rush was a notorious criminal who was executed for his involvement in the murders at Stanfield Hall in Norfolk, England. Rush was a tenant farmer of the Jermy family, who were wealthy landowners. He conducted a complex scheme to defraud the Jermy family of their property and their lives.

He murdered Isaac Jermy and his son on November 28, 1848. Rush became known as the "Killer in the Fog," as the murders took place during a thick fog that obscured visibility.

Rush had to mortgage and remortgage his farm trying to raise money to pay off his debts. However, he used the money instead to buy firearms and ammunition, which he used to murder the Jermy family. Rush had planned the murders carefully, and he had even hired a carriage to take him to the Jermy's mansion. After the murders, Rush fled the scene, but he was eventually caught.

Following his arrest, Rush was brought to trial and found guilty of the murders, and sentenced to death. On April 21, 1849, he was hanged at Norwich Castle.

After his execution a plaster copy of his death mask was made, which became part of the phrenological heads. Phrenological heads known as "murderers' row" were a set of phrenological heads [127] that were used by phrenologists to study the shape of the skull and determine the character of the person. They were part of a larger movement in the 19th century that sought to understand the human mind and behavior through the study of the brain and the skull. The phrenological heads, including the death mask of

James Bloomfield Rush, are now part of the Science Museum Group Collection.

Burke and Hare:

Fig 113

William Burke and William Hare were a notorious pair of murderers for profit who operated in the early 19th century in Edinburgh, Scotland [128]. Between November 1827 and October 1828, they are believed to have murdered at least 16 people, primarily taking destitute individuals from the streets of Edinburgh.

During the 19th century, there was a chronic shortage of cadavers for anatomy classes in Edinburgh, which gave rise to a new industry in the city: grave-robbing. However, Burke and Hare took things a step further by resorting to murder in order to obtain fresh cadavers. They targeted individuals who would not be missed and who would not be identified easily, such as travelers, prostitutes, and the destitute.

Their first victim was an army pensioner named "Old Donald", who had died owing the pair £4 in rent. Their other victims included "Daft Jamie" and the pair's last victim, Mary or Margaret Docherty, also known as "the old woman." Their modus operandi was to lure people to their lodging house, get them drunk, and then suffocate them. This preferred method left less marks on the bodies, which increased the amount that the anatomists would pay for the cadavers. After killing their victims, they sold the corpses to Robert Knox, a local anatomist, for dissection at his anatomy lectures. This, of course, eventually ended his career.

Although contemporary sources suggest that Burke was the most intelligent of the pair, it was Hare who was persuaded to turn king's evidence and accuse his partner in crime, thus escaping execution himself. Burke's trial took place on 24 December 1828, and was convicted of atrocious murder on Christmas Day. Burke was publicly hanged on January 28, 1829 in front of a crowd of 25,000 people. After his execution, his body was dissected at the medical school, and his skeleton was de-fleshed and put on display in the Anatomical Museum of Edinburgh Medical School where it remains to this day.

The death mask of William Burke was made of his shaven head after his execution. A life mask of Hare was made during his trial. Both masks have become objects of fascination for many people. Burke's death mask is on display at the University of Edinburgh's Anatomical Museum, along with his skeleton. Hare's mask, however, was lost for many years until it was discovered in a cupboard in Inveraray Jail in 2009.

In addition to their masks, other macabre artifacts associated with Burke and Hare have also survived. For example, Burke's skin was used to bind a book about his crimes, which is also on display at the Surgeons' Hall Museum. These artifacts serve as a reminder of the gruesome crimes committed by Burke and Hare, and the public fascination with their story continues to this day.

Heinrich Himmler:

Fig 114

Heinrich Himmler was a German Nazi politician, police administrator, and military commander. Born on October 7, 1900, to a middle-class family in Munich, Germany. Himmler had a strong desire to join the army, but World War I ended soon after he came of age to join the military. After the war, he studied agriculture and joined rightist paramilitary organizations. Himmler joined the Nazi Party in 1925 and rose to become head of Adolf Hitler's SS, overseeing the Nazi genocidal programs that killed millions of Jews, Romanians, and other victims.

As Reich Leader of the dreaded SS of the Nazi Party from 1929 until 1945, Himmler presided over a vast ideological and bureaucratic empire that defined him for many—both inside and outside the Third Reich—as the second most powerful man after Adolf Hitler in Germany during World War II. He obtained command of all state political police departments in Germany and centralized them within the Secret State Police (the Gestapo).

He was taken into custody on May 21, 1945, by British soldiers who had recognized him when he was wearing a non-military jacket and carrying false papers. During the interrogation, Himmler admitted his identity. On May 23, 1945, while in custody, he committed suicide by biting down on a cyanide capsule hidden in his mouth [129]. Heinrich Himmler's body was presumably buried in an unknown grave in an anonymous field by the British after his death. In 2019, a grave believed to be that of a high-ranking Nazi was dug up in Berlin, but it is unclear if it was Himmler's.

The plaster cast was made by Private Gerrans who was an RAMC (Royal Army Medical Corps) sterilizing orderly at 74th General Hospital (Luneberg). He and his Sergeant, John St George

Glyn, were detailed to measure and record Himmler's body at the scene of death, prior to transport for autopsy. The death mask is a part of the Imperial War Museum's collection and is on display for visitors to see.

Actors

David Garrick:

Fig 115

David Garrick was an English actor, producer, dramatist, poet, and co-manager of the Drury Lane Theatre. He was born on February 19, 1717, in Hereford, England, to Peter Garrick and Arabella Clough. Garrick was of French and Irish descent. His father was a captain in the English army, and his mother was the daughter of a vicar at Lichfield Cathedral who was of Irish extraction. Known as the most influential actor of his time, Garrick popularized a more natural style of acting and greatly contributed to the recognition and reverence of Shakespeare as the foremost English playwright [130].

Throughout his career, Garrick made notable contributions to the world of theater. As a talented actor, playwright, and theater manager, he had a profound impact on European theatrical practice. His efforts in promoting Shakespeare's works and his achievements as a Shakespearian actor helped put Stratford-upon-Avon on the map, particularly with his Shakespeare Jubilee.

Garrick's theatrical career began in 1741 when he appeared as Richard III at Goodman's Fields Theatre. His performance was so successful that he was immediately offered a contract by the manager of Drury Lane Theatre. Garrick's acting style was naturalistic and emotional, which contrasted with the exaggerated style of acting that was popular at the time. He became famous for his performances in Shakespearean plays such as *Hamlet, Macbeth,* and *King Lear.*

Garrick's death on January 20, 1779, was a significant event in London. His funeral was one of the largest mourning ceremonies witnessed in London until the funeral of Lord Nelson in 1805. The King and Queen were present at his home in Adelphi Terrace for a three-day mourning period before his interment at Westminster Abbey. The funeral procession included over 1,800 people who were given admission cards. A death mask was made from Garrick's face following his death, which is now cared for in the collections of the Shakespeare Birthplace Trust.

Edmund Kean:

Fig 116

Edmund Kean was born on March 17, 1789, in London, England [131]. He gained recognition as one of the greatest Shakespearean actors of the 19th century. His portrayals of villains in Shakespeare's plays were particularly notable. Kean's performances were characterized by his ability to infuse authenticity and passion into the Bard's works. He restored the originality of Shakespearean plays that had been subject to changes and censorship by previous actors.

As Kean's fame grew, so did his reputation for megalomania and ungovernable behavior. He was a turbulent genius whose personal life was fraught with controversy. In addition to his acting prowess, he was known for his short stature and tumultuous personal life, which included a controversial divorce. Kean's immense talent and tempestuous nature often created a dichotomy that added to his enigmatic allure on and off the stage.

Kean died on May 15, 1833, at his house in Richmond (then in Surrey, now in London), leaving his son Charles Kean only his name. The name proved to be a valuable asset, however, for Charles Kean became a successful actor-manager in his own right. Kean's death is described in F W Hawkins *The Life of Edmund Kean London 1869* (pp391-392): "For several hours before his death Kean was quite insensible." Throughout this period, he experienced brief lucid intervals, but ultimately succumbed to his condition.

It is unclear as to who made Kean's death mask, but it is reportedly held in the Garrick Club in the heart of London's West End theatre district founded in 1831. The gentleman's club has a large collection of theatrical memorabilia including paintings, sculptures, prints, and drawings relating to the performing arts. The club also has a library and archive which includes books and manuscripts relating to theatre history.

John Edward McCullough:

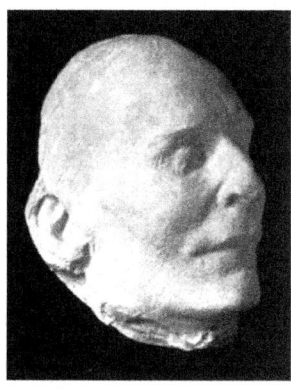

Fig 117

John Edward McCullough was born on November 14, 1837, in Coleraine, Ireland [132]. He was the second of four children born to James McCullough, and made his debut at the age of 17 in a production of *The Lady of Lyons* in New York City. McCullough quickly became a popular actor and was known for his performances in Shakespearean plays. He was also part of a company that toured America and was known for his intelligent, but not intellectual portrayal of Hamlet, which tied him to the West's working classes.

McCullough's acting career flourished during his time in the United States. He performed in various roles on both the American and British stages, displaying his talent and versatility as an actor. McCullough's popularity and skill earned him a place among the celebrated actors of his era.

McCullough died on November 8, 1885, six days after his 53rd birthday. According to theater lore, he was murdered backstage by a fellow actor and buried by members of the acting company in a cellar beneath the stage. This version of events is apocryphal and has not been substantiated.

Edwin Booth, another famous actor of the time, reportedly declined to contribute to the fund for McCullough's elaborate granite gravesite monument in Philadelphia, stating that greater actors than him, such as his own father and Edwin Forrest, had no similar monuments upon their graves.

Unhappily, mental disease preceded McCullough's death, and during the last few years of his life those who loved him best prayed for the rest which is shown on his face mask. A post-mortem examination revealed a brain of unusual size and of very high development. The death-mask was made by Mr. H. H. Kitson, of Boston.

Dion Boucicault:

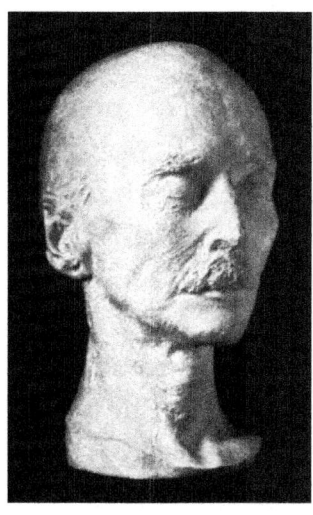

Fig 118

Dionysius Lardner "Dion" Boucicault, born on December 26, 1820, was an Irish actor and playwright renowned for his melodramas [133]. He received his education in England and began his acting career in 1837. Although his first play was rejected, his second play, *London Assurance* (1841), achieved immense success and was frequently revived well into the 20th century. Boucicault and his actress wife joined Laura Keene's theatre in 1860 and began a series of his popular Irish plays—*The Colleen Bawn*(1860), *Arrah-na-Pogue* (1864), *The O'Dowd* (1873), and *The Shaughraun* (1874). Returning to London in 1862, he provided Joseph Jefferson (actor) with a successful adaptation of *Rip Van Winkle*.

Boucicault gained popularity and acclaim for his talent in characterization and precise timing as an actor. He was also recognized for his inventive directing skills and innovative contributions as a theater manager, establishing him as one of the notable figures in Victorian theater. Throughout his lifetime, Boucicault enjoyed success on both sides of the Atlantic and was regarded as one of the most accomplished actors.

Boucicault was married three times. He married the much older Anne Guiot at St Mary-at-Lambeth on July 9, 1845. He claimed that she died in a shipwreck off the coast of Cuba in 1853, but this is not true. They separated in 1850 and she actually died in Paris in 1862. Boucicault then married Agnes Robertson, an actress who had appeared in several of his plays. They had two children together before divorcing in 1877. Boucicault's third marriage was to Louise Thorndyke, an American actress who was much younger than him. They had one child together before Boucicault's death.

Dion Boucicault, worn by age, died in the city of New York on September 18, 1890 in New York City at the age of 69. The cast of the head of Boucicault was made the day after his death, by Mr. J. Scott Hartley, of New York.

Lawrence Barrett:

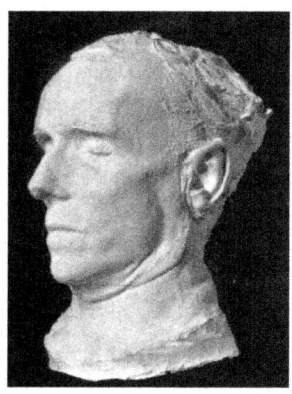

Fig 119

Lawrence Patrick Barrett was an American stage actor born on April 4, 1838, in Paterson, New Jersey, to Irish immigrants who had settled there [134]. He was raised in Detroit and made his first stage appearance there in 1853 as Murad in *The French Spy*. Barrett began his career as a member of the stock company at the Detroit Opera House and later joined the company of Edwin Forrest. He became a leading actor in the United States and England, performing in plays such as *Hamlet*, *Othello*, and *Richard III*.

Barrett began showing serious health problems in 1890. That year, after organizing performances starring Booth and Polish actress Helena Modjeska, he traveled to a spa in Germany before rejoining them in the fall. Due to a glandular problem, however, his face was swollen and his voice was weak.

Barrett died on March 20, 1891, at the age of 52 during a performance of the play *Richelieu* in New York City. The news of his death deeply affected the acting community, and actors mourned his loss. His death mask was made under the direction of Augustus Saint-Gaudens. The mask is now part of the McComas Death Mask Collection at McDaniel College Archives. Another death mask of Barrett is part of the Laurence Hutton Collection at Princeton University Library.

Edwin Booth:

Fig 120

Edwin Booth was a famous American actor born on November 13, 1833, in Bel Air, Maryland. He was the second son of Junius Brutus Booth, a well-known British actor who had immigrated to the United States.

At the age of 13, Booth became the companion and chaperon to his eccentric father [135]. Following in his father's footsteps, Edwin began his acting career and gained recognition for his talents. In 1857, he landed his first starring roles in Boston and New York City. He embarked on tours both within the United States and Europe, where he captivated audiences with his Shakespearean performances. Edwin Booth's portrayal of Hamlet, in particular, earned him widespread acclaim, and he is considered one of the greatest interpreters of the role. He holds the distinction of having portrayed Hamlet on stage more frequently than any other actor.

Tragedy struck Edwin Booth's life when his brother, John Wilkes Booth, assassinated President Abraham Lincoln in 1865. This event had a profound impact on Edwin's career and personal life. Although he was deeply affected by his brother's actions, Edwin Booth distanced himself from the assassination and focused on his acting career. He established his own theater, Booth's Theater, where he managed productions and continued to showcase his talent.

After a long career on the American stage, Booth retired from acting in 1888 and spent his declining years in his private room above The Players club that he founded. By 1893, his health had worsened considerably due to insomnia and lifelong tobacco use. In the days prior to his death, Edwin was visited by many of his acting contemporaries. One such visitor was the comedian Joseph Jefferson who found early fame by debuting as Asa Trenchard in the play *Our American Cousin* in 1858. The actor (who was actually three years older than Edwin) visited Booth two days before his death.

On June 7th, 1893, Edwin fulfilled his New Year's Eve prediction that, "You drink tonight to my health. A year from tonight you will drink to my memory." He passed away at around 1:00 o'clock in the morning – a time he had witnessed often in his solitude.

A death-mask of Booth was taken under the direction of Mr. Augustus St. Gaudens. It is kept at The Players club that he founded along with Ellen Terry's death mask and Edwin Booth's life mask.

Others

Maria F. Malibran:

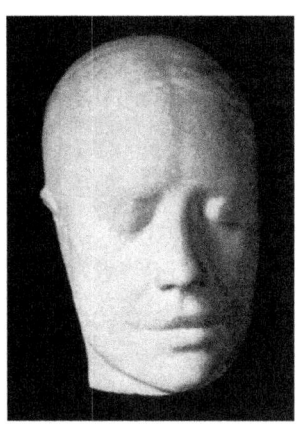

Fig 121

Maria F. Malibran, also known as Maria Felicia Malibran, was a renowned 19th-century opera singer. Born in 1808, she began her career at a young age. She first appeared on stage in Ferdinando Paër's opera *Agnese* when she was just 8 years old [136]. Recognized for her exceptional talent, she joined the choir of the King's Theatre in London when she turned 17. Malibran's powerful and expressive voice captivated audiences, establishing her as one of the most notable opera singers of her time.

Malibran was known for her stormy personality and dramatic intensity and her ability to sing both contralto and soprano parts. She performed in many operas throughout her career, including *The Barber of Seville*, *Don Giovanni*, and *Norma*. She was also known for her charity work and often performed benefit concerts for various causes.

On September 23, 1836, Malibran died in Manchester, England shortly after suffering violent convulsions at the end of a performance. She laid in a kind of stupor for several days before passing away. Her death was deeply felt by the arts community of Europe. Although a death mask was created, it is not known who created it or where it is today.

Alios Senefelder:

Fig 122

Alois Senefelder was a German inventor of lithography, born on November 6, 1771 in Prague, Czechoslovakia. He was the son of an actor at the Theatre Royal in Prague. Despite starting his studies in law at the University of Ingolstadt, Senefelder was unable to continue due to the death of his father [137]. He then pursued a career as a performer and author but faced little success. It was during this time that he developed the concept of lithography, which he first used for printing his own plays and scripts.

Lithography is a printing process that uses a flat stone or metal plate on which the image areas are worked with a greasy substance so that the ink will adhere to them, while the non-image areas are made ink-repellent. His invention made printing available to more people and was important in art and newspaper printing. Senefelder lived to see his process become widely adopted both for art printmaking and as the dominant method of pictorial reproduction in the printing industry.

Alois Senefelder passed away on February 26, 1834, in Munich, Germany, at the age of 62. The cause of his death is unspecified. Although it is not known who created his death mask, there is one believed to be authentic in the Laurence Hutton Collection at Princeton University. Also, a replica is available for purchase at Gipsformerei Berlin Online Catalogue.

Ben Caunt:

Ben Caunt was a 19th-century English bare-knuckle boxer who became the heavyweight boxing champion known as the "Torkard Giant" and "Big Ben." He was born on March 22, 1815, in Hucknall Torkard, Nottinghamshire, England. Caunt held the English heavyweight championship from 1838 to 1845. In his final fight on September 21, 1857, Caunt fought Nat Langham at Home Circuit, where after 60 rounds both men were too exhausted to continue and a draw was declared.

Outside of his boxing career, Caunt faced personal tragedies. He suffered the loss of two of his children in the Coach and Horses fire [138]. Despite these hardships, Caunt remained dedicated to his sport and continued to pursue success in the boxing world.

Caunt died of pneumonia on September 10, 1861, at an address in St Martin's Lane in London. He is buried outside the north transept of the Parish Church of St Mary Magdalene in Hucknall close to the grave of his two children.

A death mask was taken of Caunt's facial features after his death. However, it is not clear who made the death mask or where it is currently located. The Laurence Hutton Collection of Death Masks at Princeton University includes a mask of Ben Caunt, but it is not clear if this is the original mask or a copy.

L.C. La Bourdonnais:

Fig 124

Born in 1797, La Bourdonnais demonstrated his passion and talent for chess at an early age. He received guardianship from his first teacher, Jacques François Mouret, and within two years, he became one of the top players at the Café de la Régence in Paris [139]. La Bourdonnais' exceptional skills eventually led him to earn a living as a professional chess player, solidifying his status as one of the most renowned players of his time.

La Bourdonnais was particularly famous for his rivalry with the English chess master, Alexander McDonnell. The two engaged in a series of matches between 1834 and 1836, known as the

La Bourdonnais-McDonnell series, which captivated the chess world. These matches showcased La Bourdonnais' exceptional tactical skills and contributed to the development of modern chess theory.

Despite his success in chess, La Bourdonnais faced financial difficulties due to ill-advised land deals that led to the depletion of his fortune. In an attempt to secure financial stability, La Bourdonnais sought a pension from the French government. However, he passed away on December 13, 1840, before the king could grant it. Fortunately, his wife, Madame La Bourdonnais, received the pension for the remainder of her life as arranged by the Prime Minister of France, Adolphe Thiers.

In the last few weeks of his life, La Bourdonnais was entirely destitute of support due to his illness. He was suffering from an illness of a grave and complicated character that prevented him from fulfilling his professional engagement for which he left Paris. Despite his declining health, medical professionals believed that he might yet live for years, and it was certain that his chess faculty remained unimpaired until the end.

Bourdonnais died on December 13, 1840, at the age of 45. The death mask of La Bourdonnais is held in Box 25 at Princeton University's Firestone

Library. The mask was created by J. Le Ville after La Bourdonnais' death. The mask is described as "a sad caricature drawn from a dreadful mask molded after death."

Max Reinhardt:

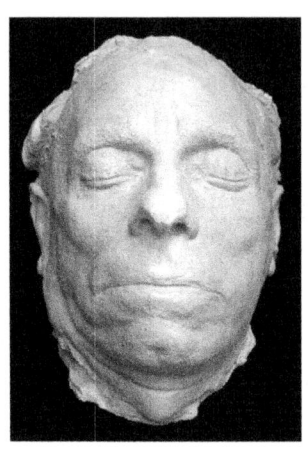

Fig 125

Max Reinhardt, born Max Goldmann, was a prominent figure in the world of theater and film. He was born on September 9, 1873, in Baden, near Vienna, Austria [140]. Reinhardt gained widespread recognition as a theatrical director, leaving a significant impact on the industry through his creative contributions.

His career was marked by notable achievements and collaborations. He directed productions in renowned venues such as the Salzburg Festival and established himself as an influential figure in European theater. Reinhardt's innovative approach to stage design, lighting, and direction revolutionized the theatrical experience and influenced subsequent generations of directors.

His involvement in film can be traced back to the 1930s when he was captured on film in his garden and seen signing a contract with the US film producer Curtis Melnitz in Berlin. His contributions to the film industry were as significant as his achievements in theater.

Reinhardt's legacy is that of a man of few words and little inclination or ability to develop or expound a dramatic theory. However, his work as a director transformed theatrical production in the 20th century. He was a pragmatist whose instinctual feelings for the rightness of things transformed theatrical production in the 20th century. Before him, the idea of the director as a creative artist in his own right had been barely embryonic. With his work, the director emerged as the dynamic formative mind behind the production of a dramatic work. Like the plots, his life was filled with lesser fortunes and poor health, and he died speechless on October 31, 1943, in New York City.

According to the Princeton University Library's Laurence Hutton Collection, Max Reinhardt's original death mask was created by Friedrich Dreyfus and is part of the collection.

Marc Isambard Brunel Sr.:

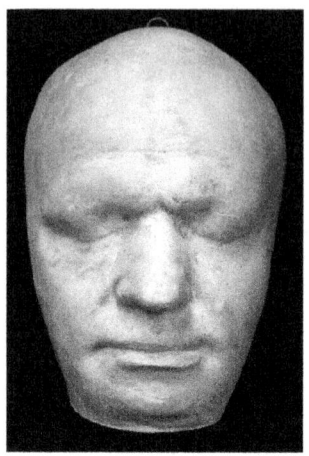

Fig 126

Brunel is best known for his remarkable achievement in solving the historic problem of underwater tunneling. Born in Hacqueville, France in April 25, 1769, Brunel initially pursued a career in the French navy, spending six years in service before returning to France in 1793 amidst the turmoil of the French Revolution [141].

He left France during the French Revolution and settled in England in 1799. In England, he became an engineer and inventor, and he developed a number of important inventions, including a machine for making pulley blocks for the Royal Navy. He also worked on the design of the Thames Tunnel, which was the first tunnel to be built under a navigable river.

Brunel's work on the Thames Tunnel was a significant achievement, but it was also a difficult and dangerous project. The tunnel was plagued by problems, including flooding, cave-ins, and financial difficulties. Brunel worked on the project for many years, and he was assisted by his son,

Isambard Kingdom Brunel. The tunnel was finally completed in 1843, and it was a major engineering achievement.

Marc Isambard Brunel Sr. passed away on December 12, 1849, in London, England. He was survived by his wife, Mary, and three children: Isambard Brunel Jr., Henry Marc Brunel, and Florence Mary Brunel. Brunel's son, Isambard Kingdom Brunel, also became a notable engineer in his own right, leaving a lasting legacy.

It is unknown as to who created Brunel's death mask. Also, there is some discrepancy about the location of the mask. One source, the New York Times, mentions that they saw the death mask at the National Portrait Gallery in London. However, another source, a blog post, does not mention the National Portrait Gallery and instead shows a photograph of a plaque at Kensal Green Cemetery in London, where Brunel is buried. There is definitely a copy of the mask in the Laurence Hutton Collection at Princeton University.

Richard Brinsley Sheridan:

Fig 127

Richard Brinsley Sheridan (1751-1816) was an Irish-born playwright, orator, and politician known for his significant contributions to British theater and politics. Born in Dublin, Ireland, Sheridan's family moved to London when he was seven years old, and he received his education at Harrow School [142].

Sheridan's career initially leaned towards a legal path, but his passion for the theater led him to pursue a career as a playwright. In 1775, his first play, *The Rivals*, was performed at London's Covent Garden Theatre, initially receiving mixed reviews but eventually establishing his reputation as a writer after revisions were made. He went on to write several other successful plays, including *The School for Scandal* and *The Critic*. Sheridan's works were highly regarded for their wit, comedic elements, and satirical commentary on societal manners and politics.

Alongside his theatrical pursuits, Sheridan was also engaged in politics. He served as a Member of Parliament (MP) for Stafford from 1780 until his death in 1816, aligning himself with the Whig party. During his political career, Sheridan held various roles, including Secretary to the Treasury and Treasurer of the Navy. He was known for utilizing his theatrical talents on the political stage, employing oratory skills to captivate audience.

Although it is not known who created his death mask, one does exist in the Laurence Hutton Collection at Princeton University.

Dolly:

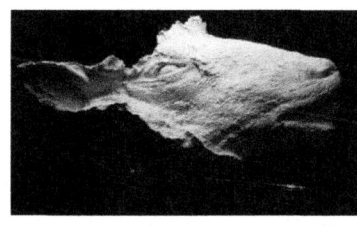

Fig 128

Dolly is one of only a few known animals to have a death mask made after its death. The first mammal to be cloned from an adult somatic cell, she was born on July 5, 1996, at the Roslin Institute in Scotland. Dolly was created using a technique called somatic cell nuclear transfer, which involves removing the nucleus from an egg cell and replacing it with the nucleus from a somatic cell. The egg is then stimulated to divide and develop into an embryo, which is implanted into a surrogate mother.

Dolly was named after the singer Dolly Parton, because the cells used to create her were taken from a mammary gland. She was a Finn-Dorset sheep, a breed known for its high fertility and good meat quality.

Her birth was a major scientific breakthrough. However, Dolly's life was not without challenges. She suffered from several health issues, including arthritis and a respiratory illness, and her shortened telomeres, which are protective caps at the ends of chromosomes, indicated that she was aging faster than normal sheep [143]. On February 14th, 2003, at the age of six, Dolly was euthanized after being diagnosed with an incurable lung tumor.

Dolly's death raised concerns about the safety of cloning and the long-term health of cloned animals. Some scientists speculated that cloning could cause premature aging and other health problems. However, subsequent studies have shown that cloned animals can live normal, healthy lives. In 2016, scientists reported that 13 other sheep clones from the same batch of cells as Dolly were aging normally, showing no signs of hypertension, diabetes, or serious arthritis at their middle age.

Dolly's death mask is a plaster cast made from a mold taken of her face after her death. It is on display at the National Museum of Scotland in

Edinburgh, along with other artifacts related to her life and legacy.

Collecting Death Masks

Collecting death masks is obviously not for everyone, but it does offer a unique opportunity to preserve the likeness of historical figures and engage with their legacies. In this summary, we will explore the process of purchasing death masks, provide cautionary advice about potential fakes, list notable death masks sold at auction, and discuss collections held by museums, universities, and individuals.

Acquiring a genuine death mask requires careful consideration and research. Here are some avenues to explore when looking to purchase one:

Auction houses often handle the sale of death masks, particularly those associated with famous individuals. Prominent auction houses such as Sotheby's and Christie's occasionally feature death masks in their sales catalog. Monitoring their upcoming auctions and reaching out to their specialists can help you find potential opportunities.

Online platforms like eBay and Etsy sometimes offer death masks for sale. However, due diligence is crucial in these cases, as there is a risk of encountering replicas or fake masks. Verify the seller's reputation, examine detailed photographs, and thoroughly research the mask's authenticity before making a purchase.

Visiting reputable antique dealers and galleries that specialize in historical artifacts may present opportunities to acquire death masks. Establishing relationships with knowledgeable dealers can provide access to a wider range of options and enhance the chances of finding genuine pieces.

Below are a few examples of notable death masks that have been sold at auction, along with their respective prices.

Ludwig van Beethoven: The death mask of the renowned composer was sold at Sotheby's in 2007 for £33,600 (approximately $45,000).

Napoleon Bonaparte: A death mask of Napoleon was sold at Sotheby's in 2005 for £169,250 (approximately $238,000).

Abraham Lincoln: A plaster cast of Lincoln's face was sold at Christie's in 2008 for $65,725. This was most likely a live mask because a mask of Lincoln was never made after his death.

When purchasing death masks, it is crucial to be aware of potential fakes in the market. Here are a few cautionary examples:

Adolf Hitler: Numerous counterfeit death masks of Adolf Hitler exist, often fabricated after World War II. These fake masks are frequently offered for sale online or in unauthorized markets. Authentic Hitler death masks do not exist, and collectors should exercise extreme caution when encountering such items.

Famous Personalities: Death masks associated with renowned figures, such as Abraham Lincoln (who only had 2 life masks made and none after death) or Albert Einstein, are frequently targeted by forgers due to their historical significance. Thoroughly researching the provenance, consulting experts, and seeking reputable sources can help authenticate these masks.

Incomplete or Replicas: Some death masks sold on the market may be incomplete or replicas. While these may still hold value for certain collectors, it is crucial to clearly understand what is being purchased and adjust expectations accordingly.

There is at least one notable purchase of a forged death mask by a museum. The Rijksmuseum in Amsterdam intentionally bought a fake death mask by master forger Han van Meegeren for €300 ($409) in 2014 at an auction in Rotterdam. The museum's director, Wim Pijbes, said that the acquisition was made to show the fallibility of museums and to complement the museum's archive of other forgeries.

Numerous museums and universities hold notable collections of death masks that may come up for sale occasionally. Here are a few examples:

The Robert Noel Collection of Life and Death Masks is a collection of 37 plaster casts made in Germany in the 19th century. The collection consists of both living and dead plaster casts. The collection is currently held at University College, London.

The Morbid Anatomy Museum in Brooklyn is a museum that showcases aspects of culture that are often dismissed as morbid or marginal. It has a private collection of over 2,000 books on medical history, death rituals, the human body, esoterica, and includes a collection of death masks.

University of Cambridge (Cambridge, United Kingdom) has a collection of death masks, including those of renowned scientists and scholars, which contribute to their academic research and historical preservation efforts.

The Laurence Hutton Collection of Life and Death Masks, housed in the Graphic Arts division of Princeton University's Firestone Library, is the largest collection of its kind in the United States.

This collection contains approximately 100 life and death masks of notable English and American figures.

Several private collectors possess collections of death masks. These collectors often acquire masks through auctions, antique dealers, or personal connections. Private collections may occasionally be made accessible through exhibitions or collaborations with museums and institutions.

In conclusion: Collecting death masks provides a glimpse into history and a tangible connection to significant individuals. When seeking to purchase a death mask, it is essential to exercise caution, research the authenticity of the mask, and consider reputable sources such as auction houses, antique dealers, and galleries. Awareness of potential fake death masks, especially those associated with famous personalities like Adolf Hitler, is crucial. Various institutions, including museums, universities, and private collectors hold remarkable collections of death masks, contributing to the preservation of historical and cultural heritage.

Conclusion

Death masks have a rich history that spans centuries and continents. From ancient Egypt to modern-day Europe, death masks have been used to preserve the likeness of the deceased and to commemorate their lives. The science of death masks has evolved over time, with advances in materials and techniques allowing for more accurate and detailed representations. The influence of death masks on art and literature is evident in the many works that have been inspired by them, from Shakespeare's *Hamlet* to the sculptures of Auguste Rodin.

Famous death masks have been created for a wide range of individuals, including royalty and nobility, military leaders, philosophers, poets, novelists, writers, musicians, scientists, chemists, doctors, composers, artists, political leaders and activists, religious leaders and notables, criminals, actors, and others. These masks provide a glimpse into the lives and personalities of those individuals, and serve as a reminder of their contributions to history.

While death masks have played an important role in preserving the memory of the deceased, they have also been the subject of controversy. Some have argued that the creation of death masks is a violation of the deceased's privacy, while others have criticized the use of death masks as a form of idolatry. Despite these criticisms, death masks continue to be created and studied, providing valuable insights into the lives and deaths of those who have come before us.

As we look to the future, it is clear that death masks will continue to play an important role in our understanding of history and culture. Advances in technology and materials will allow for even more detailed and accurate representations, while new forms of art and literature will continue to be inspired by these timeless artifacts. Whether we view death masks as a form of reverence or as a violation of privacy, there is no denying their enduring significance in the human experience.

Additional Resources

1. "Death Mask," Wikipedia
https://en.wikipedia.org/wiki/Death_mask

2. "How Death Masks Work," howstuffworks
https://science.howstuffworks.com/science-vs-myth/afterlife/death-mask3.htm

3. "A Brief Historical Overview of Death Masks since the Ancient World," Brewminate: A Bold Blend of News and Ideas
https://brewminate.com/a-brief-historical-overview-of-death-masks-since-the-ancient-world/

4. "21st Century Death Masks," death.io
https://death.io/21st-century-death-masks/

5. "Death Positive Movement," The Order of Good Death
https://www.orderofthegooddeath.com/death-positive-movement/

6. "Death Mask," Autodesk Instructables
https://www.instructables.com/Deathmask/

7. "Face Masks and Forensics," undark
https://undark.org/2016/05/19/african-face-masks-forensics/

8. "physiognomy," Britannica
https://www.britannica.com/topic/physiognomy-divination

9. "The curious and gruesome art of human death masks," CNN Style
https://www.cnn.com/style/article/death-masks/index.html

10. *Death Masks and Summary Guide*, Jim Butcher
http://www.bookrags.com/studyguide-death-masks/#gsc.tab=0

11. "Jean Antoine Houdon (1741–1828)," The Met
https://www.metmuseum.org/toah/hd/jahd/hd_jahd.htm

12. "Madame Tussaud: the astounding tale of survival behind the woman who made history," The Guardian
https://www.theguardian.com/books/2018/oct/04/madame-tussaud-edward-carey-little

13. "James De Ville," Wikipedia
https://en.wikipedia.org/wiki/James_De_Ville

14. "The Life of Thomas Woolner (1825-1892)," The Victorian Web
https://victorianweb.org/sculpture/woolner/biography.html

15. "Carlo Bartolomeo Rastrelli," Wikipedia
https://en.wikipedia.org/wiki/Carlo_Bartolomeo_Rastrelli

16. "Messerschmidt and Modernity," The J. Paul Getty Museum
https://www.getty.edu/art/exhibitions/messerschmidt/character.html

17. "Deym von Střítež, Joseph Count (1752-1804)," Mozart & Material Culture
https://mmc.kdl.kcl.ac.uk/entities/person/stritez-joseph-count-deym-von/

18. "Follow your nose – Brucciani's plaster casts of the face of Michelangelo's David as object lessons for art education," V&A
https://www.vam.ac.uk/blog/caring-for-our-collections/follow-your-nose-bruccianis-plaster-casts-of-the-face-of-michelangelos-david-as-object-lessons-for-art-education

19. "Nick Reynolds," Behind The Death Masks: Nick Reynolds: Artist / Sculptor," The Terrestrial
http://www.theterrestrial.com/interview/nick-reynolds/

20. "Henry IV of France." Wikipedia
https://en.wikipedia.org/wiki/Henry_IV_of_France

21. "Marie Louise Gonzaga," Wikipedia
https://en.wikipedia.org/wiki/Marie_Louise_Gonzaga

22. "Artist Mat Collishaw brings Queen Elizabeth I back to life with a terrifyingly lifelike animatronic mask," House&Garden
https://www.houseandgarden.co.uk/article/mat-collishaw-queen-elizabeth-i-mask

23. "Charles XII - king of Sweden," Britannica
https://www.britannica.com/biography/Charles-XII/Years-in-Turkey-1709-14

24. "Alexander I." Britannica
https://www.britannica.com/biography/Alexander-I-emperor-of-Russia

25. "Mary, Queen of Scots," Wikipedia
https://en.wikipedia.org/wiki/Mary,_Queen_of_Scots

26. "Frederick II - King of Prussia," Britannica
https://www.britannica.com/biography/Frederick-II-king-of-Prussia

27. "Louise of Prussia (1776–1810)," encyclopedia.com
https://www.encyclopedia.com/women/encyclopedias-almanacs-transcripts-and-maps/louise-prussia-1776-1810

28. "Henry VII - king of England," Britannica
https://www.britannica.com/biography/Henry-VII-king-of-England/Foreign-policy

29. "Henry Warner Slocum," Wikipedia
https://en.wikipedia.org/wiki/Henry_Warner_Slocum

30. "Honoré-Gabriel Riqueti, comte de Mirabeau - French politician and orator," Britannica
https://www.britannica.com/biography/Honore-Gabriel-Riqueti-comte-de-Mirabeau

31. "Oliver Cromwell," Historic UK
https://www.historic-uk.com/HistoryUK/HistoryofEngland/Oliver-Cromwell/

32. "George Dewey." Wikipedia
https://en.wikipedia.org/wiki/George_Dewey

33. "Józef Piłsudski - Polish revolutionary and statesman," Britannica
https://www.britannica.com/biography/Jozef-Pilsudski

34. "The death of Michael Collins – archive, 1922," The Guardian
https://www.theguardian.com/world/2022/aug/24/the-death-of-michael-collins-ireland-1922

35. "Ulysses S. Grant - THE 18TH PRESIDENT OF THE UNITED STATES," whitehouse.gov
https://www.whitehouse.gov/about-the-white-house/presidents/ulysses-s-grant/

36. "Robert E. Lee," Wikipedia
https://en.wikipedia.org/wiki/Robert_E._Lee

37. "Biography of Pancho Villa, Mexican Revolutionary," ThoughtCo
https://www.thoughtco.com/pancho-villa-1778242

38. "Death mask of William Tecumseh Sherman (1820–1891)," New York Historical Society
https://emuseum.nyhistory.org/objects/6983/death-mask-of-william-tecumseh-sherman-18201891

39. "François de Charette," Wikipedia
https://en.wikipedia.org/wiki/Fran%C3%A7ois_de_Charette

40. "The Last Days of Immanuel Kant," berfrois.com
https://www.berfrois.com/2013/03/last-days-immanuel-kant-thomas-de-quincey/

41. "Nietzsche Is Dead," Humanities
https://www.neh.gov/humanities/2012/julyaugust/feature/nietzsche-dead

42. "Giacomo Leopardi - Italian poet and philosopher," Britannica
https://www.britannica.com/biography/Giacomo-Leopardi

43. "Jeremy Bentham Biography," The Famous People
https://www.thefamouspeople.com/profiles/jeremy-bentham-307.php

44. "Edmund Burke;" Wikipedia
https://en.wikipedia.org/wiki/Edmund_Burke

45. "James Joyce Irish Author," Britannica
https://www.britannica.com/biography/James-Joyce

46. "Walt Whitman," Wikipedia
https://en.wikipedia.org/wiki/Walt_Whitman

47. "Kornel Makuszyński," Wikipedia
https://en.wikipedia.org/wiki/Kornel_Makuszy%C5%84ski

48. "Goldwin Smith," Wikipedia
https://en.wikipedia.org/wiki/Goldwin_Smith

49. "Walter Scott," Wikipedia
https://en.wikipedia.org/wiki/Walter_Scott

50. "CELIA THAXTER - Poet, Essayist And Independent Woman," History of American Women
https://www.womenhistoryblog.com/2015/07/celia-thaxter.html

51. "William Makepeace Thackeray - British author," Britannica https://www.britannica.com/biography/William-Makepeace-Thackeray

52. "Edward Kean dies at 85; head writer for 'The Howdy Doody Show'," The Los Angeles Times
https://www.latimes.com/local/obituaries/la-me-edward-kean-20100824-story.html

53. "Torquato Tasso," Britannica Kids
https://kids.britannica.com/students/article/Torquato-Tasso/277275

54. "The Life of Samuel Johnson," James Boswell, SuperSummary
https://www.supersummary.com/the-life-of-samuel-johnson/summary/

55. "William Shakespeare's Life & Times," sparknotes
https://www.sparknotes.com/shakespeare/life-and-times/

56. "Dante Alighieri," Wikipedia
https://en.wikipedia.org/wiki/Dante_Alighieri

57. "John Keats – British Poet," Britannica
https://www.britannica.com/biography/John-Keats

58. "Samuel Taylor Coleridge Biography," Encyclopedia of World Biography
https://www.notablebiographies.com/Co-Da/Coleridge-Samuel-Taylor.html

59. "Friedrich Schiller - German writer," Britannica
https://www.britannica.com/biography/Friedrich-Schiller

60. "Heinrich Heine - German author," Britannica
https://www.britannica.com/biography/Heinrich-Heine-German-author

61. "Victor Hugo - French writer," Britannica
https://www.britannica.com/biography/Victor-Hugo

62. "Carl Michael Bellman," Wikipedia
https://en.wikipedia.org/wiki/Carl_Michael_Bellman

63. "Jonathan Swift," Wikipedia
https://en.wikipedia.org/wiki/Jonathan_Swift

64. "James Hogg," Wikipedia
https://en.wikipedia.org/wiki/James_Hogg

65. "Louis Agassiz," Wikipedia
https://en.wikipedia.org/wiki/Louis_Agassiz

66. "Arthur Holly Compton - American physicist," Britannica
https://www.britannica.com/biography/Arthur-Holly-Compton

67. "Isaac Newton," Wikipedia
https://en.wikipedia.org/wiki/Isaac_Newton

68. "Alfred Nobel," Wikipedia
https://en.wikipedia.org/wiki/Alfred_Nobel

69. "Joseph Leidy - American zoologist," Britannica
https://www.britannica.com/biography/Joseph-Leidy

70. "John Hunter (surgeon)," Wikipedia
https://en.wikipedia.org/wiki/John_Hunter_(surgeon)

71. "Blaise Pascal - French philosopher and scientist," Britannica
https://www.britannica.com/biography/Blaise-Pascal

72. "Ludwig van Beethoven - German composer," Britannica
https://www.britannica.com/biography/Ludwig-van-Beethoven

73. "Felix Mendelssohn German musician and composer," Britannica
https://www.britannica.com/biography/Felix-Mendelssohn

74. "Franz Schubert," Wikipedia
https://en.wikipedia.org/wiki/Franz_Schubert

75. "Richard Wagner - German composer," Britannica
https://www.britannica.com/biography/Richard-Wagner-German-composer

76. "Franz Liszt," Biography
https://www.biography.com/musicians/franz-liszt

77. "Johann Strauss II - Austrian composer," Britannica
https://www.britannica.com/biography/Johann-Strauss-II

78. "Pyotr Ilyich Tchaikovsky - Russian composer," Britannica
https://www.britannica.com/biography/Pyotr-Ilyich-Tchaikovsky

79. "Wolfgang Mozart," Biography
https://www.biography.com/musicians/wolfgang-mozart

80. "The Life And Music Of Frederic Chopin," npr

https://www.npr.org/2011/07/18/123967818/the-life-and-music-of-frederic-chopin

81. "Josef Leopold Zvonar," peoplepill.com
https://peoplepill.com/people/josef-leopold-zvonar/

82. "Josef Moroder-Lusenberg," Wikipedia
https://en.wikipedia.org/wiki/Josef_Moroder-Lusenberg

83. "Benjamin Robert Haydon - English painter and writer," Britannica
https://www.britannica.com/biography/Benjamin-Robert-Haydon

84. "Sir Thomas Lawrence," The National Gallery
https://www.nationalgallery.org.uk/artists/sir-thomas-lawrence

85. "J. M. W. Turner," Wikipedia
https://en.wikipedia.org/wiki/J._M._W._Turner

86. "Dante_Gabriel_Rossetti," Wikipedia
https://en.wikipedia.org/wiki/Dante_Gabriel_Rossetti

87. "Wilhelm von Kaulbach," Wikipedia

https://en.wikipedia.org/wiki/Wilhelm_von_Kaulbach

88. "Antonio Canova- ITALIAN SCULPTOR," The Art Story
https://www.theartstory.org/artist/canova-antonio/

89. "John James Audubon - A complicated history," Audubon
https://www.audubon.org/content/john-james-audubon

90. "Jacques-Louis David - French painter;" Britannica
https://www.britannica.com/biography/Jacques-Louis-David-French-painter

91. "The Graphic Universe of Vojtěch Preissig," Douglass and Shuman Library & Learning Commons
https://sites.wit.edu/library/2020/11/25/the-graphic-universe-of-vojtech-preissig/

92. "Biography of Egon Schiele, Austrian Expressionist Painter," ThoughtCo
https://www.thoughtco.com/egon-schiele-biography-4177835

93. "Hiram Powers, The Greek Slave," Khan Academy
https://www.khanacademy.org/humanities/art-americas/us-art-19c/xf20f462f:us-19c-arch-sculp/a/hiram-powers-the-greek-slave

94. "THE DEATH OF NAPOLEON BONAPARTE AND THE RETOUR DES CENDRES: FRENCH AND BRITISH PERSPECTIVES," napoleon.org
https://www.napoleon.org/en/history-of-the-two-empires/articles/the-death-of-napoleon-bonaparte-and-the-retour-des-cendres-french-and-british-perspectives/

95. "Death Mask of Robert Emmet Taken by the Older Petrie," Encyclopedia Virginia
https://encyclopediavirginia.org/10957hpr-8090594917ee543/

96 "Joseph Stalin," Biography
https://www.biography.com/political-figures/joseph-stalin

97. "Thomas Paine," Biography
https://www.biography.com/political-figures/thomas-paine

98. "Aaron Burr, Staten Island, and the tale of his death mask," bowryboyshistory.com
https://www.boweryboyshistory.com/2012/01/aaron-burr-staten-island-and-tale-of.html

99. "Daniel O'Connell - Irish leader," Britannica
https://www.britannica.com/biography/Daniel-OConnell

100. "William McKinley - president of United States," Britannica
https://www.britannica.com/biography/William-McKinley

101. "Theodore Roosevelt - president of United States," Britannica
https://www.britannica.com/biography/Theodore-Roosevelt

102. "Vladimir Lenin," Biography
https://www.biography.com/political-figures/vladimir-lenin

103. "Biography of Lorenzo de' Medici," ThoughtCo
https://www.thoughtco.com/biography-of-lorenzo-de-medici-4588616

104. "Eva Perón," Biography
https://www.biography.com/political-figures/eva-peron

105. "John Philpot Curran," Wikipedia
https://en.wikipedia.org/wiki/John_Philpot_Curran

106. "Lord Palmerston - prime minister of United Kingdom," Britannica https://www.britannica.com/biography/Henry-John-Temple-3rd-Viscount-Palmerston

107. "Benjamin Disraeli - prime minister of United Kingdom;" Britannica
https://www.britannica.com/biography/Benjamin-Disraeli/Conservative-leader

108. "Daniel Webster," History
https://www.history.com/topics/19th-century/daniel-webster

109. "Assassination of Marat," World History Encyclopedia
https://www.worldhistory.org/article/2092/assassination-of-marat/

110. "George, Henry - BIBLIOGRAPHY," enclycopedia.com
https://www.encyclopedia.com/people/social-sciences-and-law/economics-biographies/henry-george

111. "Camillo Benso, Count of Cavour," Wikipedia
https://en.wikipedia.org/wiki/Camillo_Benso,_Count_of_Cavour

112. "Charles Sumner," Wikipedia
https://en.wikipedia.org/wiki/Charles_Sumner

113. "Maximilien de Robespierre." Biography
https://www.biography.com/political-figures/maximilien-de-robespierre

114. "How Did Martin Luther Die?" igonier.org
https://www.ligonier.org/learn/articles/martin-luthers-death-and-legacy

115. "Martin Luther King, Jr. - American religious leader and civil-rights activist," Britannica
https://www.britannica.com/biography/Martin-Luther-King-Jr

116. "Biography of St. Ignatius Loyola
Early Life of St. Ignatius," Loyola University, Chicago
https://www.luc.edu/mission/archivedjesuitpages/jesuitcommunityatloyolauniversitychicago/biographyofstignatiusloyola/

117. "Biography of Jose Maria Morelos, Mexican Revolutionary," ThoughtCo
https://www.thoughtco.com/jose-maria-morelos-2136464

118. "Pope Pius IX," New Advent

263

https://www.newadvent.org/cathen/12134b.htm

119. "Thomas Chalmers, 1780-1847," The History of Economic Thought
https://www.hetwebsite.net/het/profiles/chalmers.htm
https://en.wikipedia.org/wiki/Dante_Gabriel_Rossetti

120. "Harry Edwards (healer)," Wikipedia
https://en.wikipedia.org/wiki/Harry_Edwards_(healer)

121. "Who Killed Joseph Smith?" The Church of Jesus Christ
https://history.churchofjesuschrist.org/content/museum/museum-treasures-powder-horn?lang=eng

122. "The Case of Sacco and Vanzetti," The Atlantic
https://www.theatlantic.com/magazine/archive/1927/03/the-case-of-sacco-and-vanzetti/306625/

123. "Ned Kelly: The outlaw who divides a nation," BBC News
https://www.bbc.com/news/magazine-21077457

124. "Richard Parker (mutineer)," Wikipedia
https://en.wikipedia.org/wiki/Richard_Parker_(mutineer)

125. "Palmer the Poisoner," Science History Institute
https://www.sciencehistory.org/distillations/palmer-the-poisoner

126. "John Dillinger." fbi.gov
https://www.fbi.gov/history/famous-cases/john-dillinger

127. "James Bloomfield Rush Painted plaster death mask of James Bloomfield Rush, England," Europeana
https://www.europeana.eu/en/item/9200579/madst27c

128. "Burke and Hare," The University of Edinburgh
https://www.ed.ac.uk/medicine-vet-medicine/about/history/burke-and-hare

129. "Heinrich Himmler," Wikipedia
https://en.wikipedia.org/wiki/Heinrich_Himmler

130. "David Garrick," Shakespeare birthplace trust
https://www.shakespeare.org.uk/explore-shakespeare/shakespedia/david-garrick/

131. "Edmund Kean," Wikipedia

https://en.wikipedia.org/wiki/Edmund_Kean

132. "John McCullough (actor)," Wikipedia
https://en.wikipedia.org/wiki/John_McCullough_(actor)

133. "Dion Boucicault," Wikipedia
https://en.wikipedia.org/wiki/Dion_Boucicault

134. "Lawrence Barrett - American actor," Britannica
https://www.britannica.com/biography/Lawrence-Barrett

135. "Edwin Booth - American actor," Britannica
https://www.britannica.com/biography/Edwin-Booth

136. "Maria Malibran 1808-1836," Graphic Arts Collection, Special Collections, Firestone Library, Princeton University
https://graphicarts.princeton.edu/2021/01/12/maria-malibran-1808-1836/

137. "Alois Senefelder - German lithographer," Britannica
https://www.britannica.com/technology/lithography

138. "Ben Caunt," Wikipedia
https://en.wikipedia.org/wiki/Ben_Caunt

139. "Louis-Charles Mahé de La Bourdonnais," Wikipedia
https://en.wikipedia.org/wiki/Louis-Charles_Mah%C3%A9_de_La_Bourdonnais

140. "Max Reinhardt," enclyclopedia.com
https://www.encyclopedia.com/people/literature-and-arts/theater-biographies/max-reinhardt

141. "Sir Marc Isambard Brunel - French-British engineer," Britannica
https://www.britannica.com/biography/Marc-Isambard-Brunel

142. "Richard Brinsley Sheridan - Anglo-Irish playwright," Britannica
https://www.britannica.com/biography/Richard-Brinsley-Sheridan

143. "Dolly (sheep)," Wikipedia
https://en.wikipedia.org/wiki/Dolly_(sheep)

Image References

Licenses:
GNU Free Documentation
https://commons.wikimedia.org/wiki/Commons GNU_Free_Documentation_License,_version_1.2
Public Domain
https://en.wikipedia.org/wiki/Public_domain
Creative Commons (CC)
https://creativecommons.org/about/cclicenses/

Fig 1
File:Tutanchamun Maske.jpg, Wikipedia
Author: MykReeve, License: GNU Free Documentation License, Ver. 1.2
https://commons.wikimedia.org/wiki/File:Tutanchamun_Maske.jpg

Fig 2
File:Gold death-mask known as 'Mask of Agamemnon,' Mycenae, Grave Circle A, Grave V, 16th cent. BC. (28423089016).jpg
Author: Gary Todd, License: CC-01 Public Domain
https://commons.wikimedia.org/wiki/File:Gold_death-mask_known_as_%E2%80%98Mask_of_Agamemnon,%E2%80%99_Mycenae,_Grave_Circle_A,_Grave_V,_16th_cent._BC._(28423089016).jpg

Fig 3
File:Making Death Mask Edit 3.jpg
Source: George Grantham Bain - Library of Congress
License: Public Domain
https://commons.wikimedia.org/wiki/File:Making_Death_Mask_Edit_3.jpg

Fig 4
File:James Ensor - Masks Mocking Death.jpg
Source: Museum of Modern Art, License: Public Domain, CC-USA
https://commons.wikimedia.org/wiki/File:James_Ensor_-_Masks_Mocking_Death.jpg

Fig 5
"Henry IV of France," *Portraits in Plaster* by Laurence Hutton
https://www.gutenberg.org/files/52730/52730-h/52730-h.htm

Fig 6
File:Death mask of Marie Louise Gonzaga.jpg
Source/Photographer: Bożena Fabiani, License: Public Domain
https://commons.wikimedia.org/wiki/File:Death_mask_of_Marie_Louise_Gonzaga.jpg

Fig 7
"Elizabeth I, Queen of England, 1533-1603," Laurence Hutton Collection
Source: Curtesy of Princeton University

Fig 8
File:CharlesXII mummy with Death mask.jpg
Author: photographer Otto Mattson, License: Public Domain
https://commons.wikimedia.org/wiki/File:CharlesXII_mummy_with_Death_mask.jpg

Fig 9
File:Death mask tsar alex.jpg, Author: shako
License: CC Attribution-Share Alike 3.0 Unported
https://commons.wikimedia.org/wiki/File:Death_mask_tsar_alex.jpg

Fig 10
File:Queen Mary death mask copy, Falkland Palace.JPG
Author: Kim Trayor, License: CC Attribution-Share Alike 3.0 Unported
https://commons.wikimedia.org/wiki/File:Queen_Mary_death_mask_copy,_Falkland_Palace.JPG

Fig 11
File:Frederick's death mask.gif, Source: http://friedrich.uni-trier.de/de/volz/7/uc_p14/
License: Public Domain
https://commons.wikimedia.org/wiki/File:Frederick%27s_death_mask.gif

Fig 12
"Louise of Prussia," *Portraits in Plaster* by Laurence Hutton
https://www.gutenberg.org/files/52730/52730-h/52730-h.htm

Fig 13
File:Henry VII of England death mask.jpg, Author: Unknown
License: Public Domain

https://commons.wikimedia.org/wiki/File:Henry_VII_of_England_death_mask.jpg

Fig 14
"Slocum, Henry Warner, 1827-1894," Laurence Hutton Collection
Source: Curtesy of Princeton University

Fig 15
"G. R. Mirabeau," *Portraits in Plaster* by Laurence Hutton
https://www.gutenberg.org/files/52730/52730-h/52730-h.htm

Fig 16
File:Oliver Cromwell's death mask MOX.jpg
Author: The History Wizard of Cambridge
License: CC CC0 1.0 Universal Public Domain Dedication
https://commons.wikimedia.org/wiki/File:Oliver_Cromwell%27s_death_mask_MOX.jpg

Fig 17
File:DUNBAR, U.S.J. WITH DEATH MASK OF ADMIRAL DEWEY LCCN2016867538.jpg
Author: Harris & Ewing, photographer
License: Public Domain, Library of Congress
https://commons.wikimedia.org/wiki/File:DUNBAR,_U.S.J._WITH_DEATH_MASK_OF_ADMIRAL_DEWEY_LCCN2016867538.jpg

Fig 18
File:Death Mask of Marshal of Poland Józef Piłsudski.PNG
Author: Anonymous, License: CC Attribution-Share Alike 3.0 Unported
https://commons.wikimedia.org/wiki/File:Death_Mask_of_Marshal_of_Poland_J%C3%B3zef_Pi%C5%82sudski.PNG

Fig 19
File:The death mask of Michael Collins.jpg
Author: Alber Power, License: CC Attribution-Share Alike 4.0 International
https://commons.wikimedia.org/wiki/File:The_death_mask_of_Michael_Collins.jpg

Fig 20
File:Ulysses S. Grant death mask Gerhardt.jpg
Author: Karl Gerhardt, License: Public Domain

https://commons.wikimedia.org/wiki/File:Ulysses_S._Grant_death_mask_Gerhardt.jpg

Fig 21
File:Leedeathmask.jpg, Author: Daniel Hass, License: Public Domain
https://commons.wikimedia.org/wiki/File:Leedeathmask.jpg

Fig 22
File:Pancho Villas Death Mask (11199646203).jpg
Author: Karen Neoh, License: CC Attribution 2.0 Generic
https://commons.wikimedia.org/wiki/File:Pancho_Villas_Death_Mask_(11199646203).jpg

Fig 23
File:Shermandeathmask.jpg, Author: Daniel Hass
License: Public Domain
https://commons.wikimedia.org/wiki/File:Shermandeathmask.jpg

Fig 24
File:Historial - Charette mask.jpg
Author: Shelbymay, License: CC Attribution-Share Alike 3.0 Unported
https://commons.wikimedia.org/wiki/File:Historial_-_Charette_mask.jpg

Fig 25
File:Kant totenmaske 1.jpg, Author: Andreas Knorre
License: Public Domain
https://commons.wikimedia.org/wiki/File:Kant_totenmaske_1.jpg

Fig 26
File:Thielska galleriet, Nietzsches dödsmask, 2016.jpg
Author: Holger Eligaard, License: CC Attribution-Share Alike 4.0 International
https://commons.wikimedia.org/wiki/File:Thielska_galleriet,_Nietzsches_d%C3%B6dsmask,_2016.jpg

Fig 27
"Leopardi, Giacomo, 1798-1837," Laurence Hutton Collection
Source: Curtesy of Princeton University

Fig 28
"JEREMY BENTHAM," *Portraits in Plaster* by Laurence Hutton

https://www.gutenberg.org/files/52730/52730-h/52730-h.htm

Fig 29
"Edmund Burke," *Portraits in Plaster* by Laurence Hutton
https://www.gutenberg.org/files/52730/52730-h/52730-h.htm

Fig 30
File:James Joyce death mask.jpg, Author: Rrburke
License: CC Attribution-Share Alike 4.0 International
https://commons.wikimedia.org/wiki/File:James_Joyce_death_mask.jpg

Fig 31
"Whitman, Walt, 1819-1892," Laurence Hutton Collection
Source: Curtesy of Princeton University

Fig 32
File:Death mask of Kornel Makuszyński.JPG
Author: Anonymous, License: GNU Free Documentation License, Ver1.2
https://commons.wikimedia.org/wiki/File:Death_mask_of_Kornel_Makuszy%C5%84ski.JPG

Fig 33
File:Death-Mask of Goldwin Smith.jpg
Author: Unknown, License: Public Domain
https://commons.wikimedia.org/wiki/File:Death-Mask_of_Goldwin_Smith.jpg

Fig 34
"Sir Walter Scott," *Portraits in Plaster* by Laurence Hutton
https://www.gutenberg.org/files/52730/52730-h/52730-h.htm

Fig 35
"Thaxter, Celia, 1835-1894," Laurence Hutton Collection
Source: Curtesy of Princeton University

Fig 36
"William Makepeace Thackery," *Portraits in Plaster* by Laurence Hutton
https://www.gutenberg.org/files/52730/52730-h/52730-h.htm

Fig 37
"Kean, Edward, 1787-1833," Laurence Hutton Collection
Source: Curtesy of Princeton University

Fig 38
"Torquato Tasso," *Portraits in Plaster* by Laurence Hutton
https://www.gutenberg.org/files/52730/52730-h/52730-h.htm

Fig 39
"Samual Johnson," *Portraits in Plaster* by Laurence Hutton
https://www.gutenberg.org/files/52730/52730-h/52730-h.htm

Fig 40
File:The death mask of Shakespeare (IA deathmaskofshake00norr) (page 6 face crop 2).jpg
Author: Norris, Joseph Parker, License: Public Domain
https://commons.wikimedia.org/wiki/File:The_death_mask_of_Shakespeare_(IA_deathmaskofshake00norr)_(page_6_face_crop_2).jpg

Fig 41
File:Appartamento dei priori, maschera di dante (falso dei primi del novecento).JPG
Author: Saiko, License: CC Attribution-Share Alike 3.0 Unported
https://commons.wikimedia.org/wiki/File:Appartamento_dei_priori,_maschera_di_dante_(falso_dei_primi_del_novecento).JPG

Fig 42
File:The death mask of John Keats.jpg, Author: Stephencdickson
License: CC Attribution-Share Alike 4.0 International
https://commons.wikimedia.org/wiki/File:The_death_mask_of_John_Keats.jpg

Fig 43
"Coleridge, Samuel Taylor, 1772-1834," Laurence Hutton Collection
Source: Curtesy of Princeton University

Fig 44
File:Friedrich Schiller - Totenmaske 001.jpg
Author: The Public Domain Review, License: Public Domain
https://commons.wikimedia.org/wiki/File:Friedrich_Schiller_-_Totenmaske_001.jpg

Fig 45
"Heine, Heinrich, 1797-1856," Laurence Hutton Collection
Source: Curtesy of Princeton University

Fig 46
File:Dalou Victor Hugo.jpg, Author: Siren-Com

License: CC Attribution-Share Alike 3.0 Unported
https://commons.wikimedia.org/wiki/File:Dalou_Victor_Hugo.jpg

Fig 47
File:Bellman death mask Sweden.jpg, Author: Sven Rosborn
License: GNU Free Documentation License, Version 1.2
https://commons.wikimedia.org/wiki/File:Bellman_death_mask_Sweden.jpg

Fig 48
File:Jonathan Swift death mask.jpg, Author: Davepape
License: CC CC0 1.0 Universal Public Domain Dedication
https://commons.wikimedia.org/wiki/File:Jonathan_Swift_death_mask.jpg

Fig 49
File:James Hogg death mask.JPG
Author: Kim Traynor, License: CC Attribution-Share Alike 3.0 Unported
https://commons.wikimedia.org/wiki/File:James_Hogg_death_mask.JPG

Fig 50
"LOUIS AGASSIZ—From Death," *Portraits in Plaster* by Laurence Hutton
https://www.gutenberg.org/files/52730/52730-h/52730-h.htm

Fig 51
"Compton, Arthur H., 1892-1962," Laurence Hutton Collection
Source: Curtesy of Princeton University

Fig 52
File:NewtonDeathMask.jpg, Author: Adhemarius
License: CC Attribution-Share Alike 3.0 Unported
https://commons.wikimedia.org/wiki/File:NewtonDeathMask.jpg

Fig 53
File:Alfred Nobel Death mask.jpg, Author: Heinz-Josef Lücking
License: CC Attribution-Share Alike 3.0 Germany
https://commons.wikimedia.org/wiki/File:Alfred_Nobel_Death_mask.jpg

Fig 54
"Leidy, Joseph, 1823-1891," Laurence Hutton Collection
Source: Curtesy of Princeton University

Fig 55
File:The death mask of Dr John Hunter, Hunterian Art Gallery, Glasgow.jpg
Author: Stephencdickson, License: CC Attribution-Share Alike 4.0 International
https://commons.wikimedia.org/wiki/File:The_death_mask_of_Dr_John_Hunter,_Hunterian_Art_Gallery,_Glasgow.jpg

Fig 56
File:Masque mortuaire de Blaise Pascal, 1662, Bibliothèque de la Société de Port-Royal - Exposition Blaise Pascal à la Bibliothèque nationale de France (2).jpg
Author: ActuaLitte, License: CC Attribution-Share Alike 2.0 Generic
https://commons.wikimedia.org/wiki/File:Masque_mortuaire_de_Blaise_Pascal,_1662,_Biblioth%C3%A8que_de_la_Soci%C3%A9t%C3%A9_de_Port-Royal_-_Exposition_Blaise_Pascal_%C3%A0_la_Biblioth%C3%A8que_nationale_de_France_(2).jpg

Fig 57
File:Beethovendeathmask.jpg, Author: Daniel Hass
License: Public Domain
https://commons.wikimedia.org/wiki/File:Beethovendeathmask.jpg

Fig 58
"Felix Mendelssohn," *Portraits in Plaster* by Laurence Hutton
https://www.gutenberg.org/files/52730/52730-h/52730-h.htm

Fig 59
File:Schubert-Totenmaske.tif.jpg
Author: SCHUBERTcommons, License: CC Attribution-Share Alike 3.0 Unported
https://commons.wikimedia.org/wiki/File:Schubert-Totenmaske.tif

Fig 60
File:Bayreuth Richard Wagner-Totenmaske, Haus Wahnfried.jpg
Author: Bayreuth2009
License: GNU Free Documentation License, Version 1.2
https://commons.wikimedia.org/wiki/File:Bayreuth_Richard_Wagner-Totenmaske,_Haus_Wahnfried.jpg

Fig 61
File:Liszt Totenmaske.JPG, Author: Hermann Junghans
License: CC Attribution-Share Alike 3.0 Unported
https://commons.wikimedia.org/wiki/File:Liszt_Totenmaske.JPG

Fig 62
File:Austria-02832 - Death Mask (32088925734).jpg
Author: Dennis Jarvis, License: CC Attribution-Share Alike 2.0 Generic
https://commons.wikimedia.org/wiki/File:Austria-02832_-_Death_Mask_(32088925734).jpg

Fig 63
File:Tchaikovskydeathmask.jpg
Author: Daniel Hass, License: Public Domain
https://commons.wikimedia.org/wiki/File:Tchaikovskydeathmask.jpg

Fig 64
File:DeathMaskMozart.jpg, Author: Unauthenticated, unknown Artist License: Public Domain, CC-USA
https://commons.wikimedia.org/wiki/File:DeathMaskMozart.jpg

Fig 65
File:Chopin death mask, side view (collection of Jack Gibbons).jpg
Author: Jack Gibbons Pianist
License: CC Attribution-Share Alike 3.0 Unported
https://commons.wikimedia.org/wiki/File:Chopin_death_mask,_side_view_(collection_of_Jack_Gibbons).jpg

Fig 66
File:Zvonar death mask.jpg
Author: Jakub Hauser, License: CC Attribution 4.0 International
https://commons.wikimedia.org/wiki/File:Zvonar_death_mask.jpg

Fig 67
File:Josef Moroder Lusenberg death mask.JPG
Author: Wolfgang Moroder, License: CC Attribution-Share Alike 3.0 Unported
https://commons.wikimedia.org/wiki/File:Josef_Moroder_Lusenberg_death_mask.JPG

Fig 68
"Benjamin Robert Hayden," *Portraits in Plaster* by Laurence Hutton

https://www.gutenberg.org/files/52730/52730-h/52730-h.htm

Fig 69
"Sir Thomas Lawrence," *Portraits in Plaster* by Laurence Hutton
https://www.gutenberg.org/files/52730/52730-h/52730-h.htm

Fig 70
"J. M. W. Turner," *Portraits in Plaster* by Laurence Hutton
https://www.gutenberg.org/files/52730/52730-h/52730-h.htm

Fig 71
"Dante Gabriel Rossetti," *Portraits in Plaster* by Laurence Hutton
https://www.gutenberg.org/files/52730/52730-h/52730-h.htm

Fig 72
"Kaulback, Wilhelm von, 1805-1874," Laurence Hutton Collection
Source: Curtesy of Princeton University

Fig 73
"Antonio Canova," *Portraits in Plaster* by Laurence Hutton
https://www.gutenberg.org/files/52730/52730-h/52730-h.htm

Fig 74
"Audubon, John James, 1785-1851," Laurence Hutton Collection
Source: Curtesy of Princeton University

Fig 75
File:Death mask of Jacques-Louis David, 1825.JPG
Author: StephenDickson
License: CC Attribution-Share Alike 4.0 International
https://commons.wikimedia.org/wiki/File:Death_mask_of_Jacques-Louis_David,_1825.JPG

Fig 76
File:Vojtech Preissig death mask.jpg
Author: 6M52AED73UK5DPG9D, License: CC Attribution-Share Alike 4.0 International
https://commons.wikimedia.org/wiki/File:Vojtech_Preissig_death_mask.jpg

Fig 77
File:SCHIELE Totenmaske.JPG
Author: Leopold Museum / Foto: Dir. Weinhäupl
License: Public Domain

https://commons.wikimedia.org/wiki/File:SCHIELE_Totenmaske.JPG

Fig 78
Death Mask of Hiram Powers, Smithsonian American Art Museum
Authors: Thomas Ball, Joel Tanner Hart
License: no copyright reserved
https://americanart.si.edu/artwork/death-mask-hiram-powers-20127

Fig 79
File:Death mask of Napoleon-IMG 1535-black.jpg
Author: Rama, License: CC Attribution-Share Alike 2.0 France
https://commons.wikimedia.org/wiki/File:Death_mask_of_Napoleon-IMG_1535-black.jpg

Fig 80
File:Robert Emmet death mask only.jpg
Author: David M. Jensen, License: CC Attribution-Share Alike 3.0 Unported
https://commons.wikimedia.org/wiki/File:Robert_Emmet_death_mask_only.jpg

Fig 81
File:Joseph Stalin death mask in Gori Stalin Museum (14832071138).jpg
Author: Gill M.L., License: CC Attribution-Share Alike 2.0 Generic
https://commons.wikimedia.org/wiki/File:Joseph_Stalin_death_mask_in_Gori_Stalin_Museum_(14832071138).jpg

Fig 82
File:Thomas Paine death mask.jpg
Author: Hammersfan, License: CC Attribution-Share Alike 4.0 International
https://commons.wikimedia.org/wiki/File:Thomas_Paine_death_mask.jpg

Fig 83
File:WLA nyhistorical Aaron Burr.jpg
Author: Wikipedia Loves Art participant "team_coi"
License: CC Attribution-Share Alike 2.5 Generic
https://commons.wikimedia.org/wiki/File:WLA_nyhistorical_Aaron_Burr.jpg

Fig 84

File:Daniel O'Connell. Death Mask.jpg, Author: Spring To Life
License: CC Attribution-Share Alike 4.0 International
https://commons.wikimedia.org/wiki/File:Daniel_O%27Connell._Death_Mask.jpg

Fig 85
File:WilliamMcKinleysDeathMask.jpg
Author: DCPL Commons, License: Public Domain
https://commons.wikimedia.org/wiki/File:WilliamMcKinleysDeathMask.jpg

Fig 86
File:Bronze Death Mask of Theodore Roosevelt (1be40c80-6bfb-45ab-ba98-b5abbc4b819a).JPG
Source: NPGallery, License: Public Domain
https://commons.wikimedia.org/wiki/File:Bronze_Death_Mask_of_Theodore_Roosevelt_(1be40c80-6bfb-45ab-ba98-b5abbc4b819a).JPG

Fig 87
File:Lenin-halottimaszk.JPG
Source/Photographer: Brendel Matyas, License: CC Attribution-Share Alike 1.0 Generic
https://commons.wikimedia.org/wiki/File:Lenin-halottimaszk.JPG

Fig 88
File:Lorenzo death mask.jpg
Source/Photographer: http://4.bp.blogspot.com/Laura
License: CC Attribution-Share Alike 4.0 International
https://commons.wikimedia.org/wiki/File:Lorenzo_death_mask.jpg

Fig 89
File:A cast of the death mask of Eva Peron, aka Evita, at Buenos Aires' Evita Museum (15940615601).png
Author: Tim Adams, License: CC Attribution 2.0 Generic
https://commons.wikimedia.org/wiki/File:A_cast_of_the_death_mask_of_Eva_Peron,_aka_Evita,_at_Buenos_Aires%27_Evita_Museum_(15940615601).png

Fig 90
"John Philpot Curran," *Portraits in Plaster* by Laurence Hutton
https://www.gutenberg.org/files/52730/52730-h/52730-h.htm

Fig 91
"Lord Palmerston," *Portraits in Plaster* by Laurence Hutton
https://www.gutenberg.org/files/52730/52730-h/52730-h.htm

Fig 92
"Benjamin Disraeli," *Portraits in Plaster* by Laurence Hutton
https://www.gutenberg.org/files/52730/52730-h/52730-h.htm

Fig 93
"Daniel Webster," *Portraits in Plaster* by Laurence Hutton
https://www.gutenberg.org/files/52730/52730-h/52730-h.htm

Fig 94
"Marat, Jean Paul, 1743-1793," Laurence Hutton Collection
Source: Curtesy of Princeton University

Fig 95
"George, Henry, 1839-1897," Laurence Hutton Collection
Source: Curtesy of Princeton University

Fig 96
"Count Cavour," *Portraits in Plaster* by Laurence Hutton
https://www.gutenberg.org/files/52730/52730-h/52730-h.htm

Fig 97
"Charles Sumner," *Portraits in Plaster* by Laurence Hutton
https://www.gutenberg.org/files/52730/52730-h/52730-h.htm

Fig 98
"MAXIMILIAN ROBESPIERRE," *Portraits in Plaster* by Laurence Hutton
https://www.gutenberg.org/files/52730/52730-h/52730-h.htm

Fig 99
File:Luther death-hand mask.jpg, Author: Photograph by Paul T. McCain
License: CC Attribution-Share Alike 2.5 Generic
https://commons.wikimedia.org/wiki/File:Luther_death-hand_mask.jpg

Fig 100
File:Martin Luther King Jrs Death Mask (11199518704).jpg
Author: Karen Neoh, License: CC Attribution 2.0 Generic
https://commons.wikimedia.org/wiki/File:Martin_Luther_King_Jrs_Death_Mask_(11199518704).jpg

Fig 101
File:Curia of the Society of Jesus archives, death mask of St Ignatius, Rome (28941782637).jpg
Author: PjpoSullivan1, License: CC Attribution-Share Alike 2.0 Generic
https://commons.wikimedia.org/wiki/File:Curia_of_the_Society_of_Jesus_archives,_death_mask_of_St_Ignatius,_Rome_(28941782637).jpg

Fig 102
File:Death Mask of Jose Maria Morelos - Museo Casa de Morelos - Morelia - Michoacan - Mexico (20497156755).jpg
Author: Adam Jones, License: CC Attribution-Share Alike 2.0 Generic
https://commons.wikimedia.org/wiki/File:Death_Mask_of_Jose_Maria_Morelos_-_Museo_Casa_de_Morelos_-_Morelia_-_Michoacan_-_Mexico_(20497156755).jpg

Fig 103
"Pope Pius IX," *Portraits in Plaster* by Laurence Hutton
https://www.gutenberg.org/files/52730/52730-h/52730-h.htm

Fig 104
"Thomas Chalmers," *Portraits in Plaster* by Laurence Hutton
https://www.gutenberg.org/files/52730/52730-h/52730-h.htm

Fig 105
"Edwards, Harry, 1830-1891," Laurence Hutton Collection
Source: Curtesy of Princeton University

Fig 106
File:Death masks of Joseph and Hyrum Smith.png
Author: Kenneth R. Mays
License: CC0 1.0 Universal Public Domain Dedication
https://commons.wikimedia.org/wiki/File:Death_masks_of_Joseph_and_Hyrum_Smith.png

Fig 107
Sacco Vanzetti death masks - front view - Sacco & Vanzetti collection
Source: Boston Public Library, License: Public Domain
https://picryl.com/media/sacco-vanzetti-death-masks-front-view-ff50e7

Fig 108
File:Death Mask of Ned Kelly - www.joyofmuseums.com - Old Melbourne Gaol.jpg, Author: joyofmuseums
License: CC Attribution-Share Alike 4.0 International
https://commons.wikimedia.org/wiki/File:Death_Mask_of_Ned_Kelly_-_www.joyofmuseums.com_-_Old_Melbourne_Gaol.jpg

Fig 109
File:Death mask of Richard Parker.jpg, Author: Baldovio
License: CC Attribution-Share Alike 4.0 International
https://commons.wikimedia.org/wiki/File:Death_mask_of_Richard_Parker.jpg

Fig 110
File:William Palmer (murderer) death mask.jpg, Wikipedia
Author: Lithograph after Moritz Krantz and Bernard Hollander
License: CC Attribution 4.0 International
https://en.wikipedia.org/wiki/File:William_Palmer_(murderer)_death_mask.jpg

Fig 111
File:National Museum of Crime and Punishment - John Dillinger death mask (2873598482).jpg
Author: David from Washington D.C.
License: CC Attribution 2.0 Generic
https://commons.wikimedia.org/wiki/File:National_Museum_of_Crime_and_Punishmen_-_John_Dillinger_death_mask_(2873598482).jpg

Fig 112
File:Painted plaster death mask of James Bloomfield Rush, England Wellcome L0057556.jpg
Source/Photographer: Wellcome Images
License: Attribution 4.0 International
https://commons.wikimedia.org/wiki/File:Painted_plaster_death_mask_of_James_Bloomfield_Rush,_England_Wellcome_L0057556.jpg

Fig 113
File:The death masks of Burke and Hare.jpg, Author: Stephencdickson
License: CC Attribution-Share Alike 4.0 International

https://commons.wikimedia.org/wiki/File:The_death_masks_of_Burke_and_Hare.jpg

Fig 114
File:Himmler-death-mask.jpg, Author: Franks Valli
License: Public Domain
https://commons.wikimedia.org/wiki/File:Himmler-death-mask.jpg

Fig 115
"David Garrick" *Portraits in Plaster* by Laurence Hutton
https://www.gutenberg.org/files/52730/52730-h/52730-h.htm

Fig 116
"Edmund Kean," *Portraits in Plaster* by Laurence Hutton
https://www.gutenberg.org/files/52730/52730-h/52730-h.htm

Fig 117
"JOHN M'CULLOUGH," *Portraits in Plaster* by Laurence Hutton
https://www.gutenberg.org/files/52730/52730-h/52730-h.htm

Fig 118
"Dion Boucicault," *Portraits in Plaster* by Laurence Hutton
https://www.gutenberg.org/files/52730/52730-h/52730-h.htm

Fig 119
"Lawrence Barrett," *Portraits in Plaster* by Laurence Hutton
https://www.gutenberg.org/files/52730/52730-h/52730-h.htm

Fig 120
"Edwin Booth," *Portraits in Plaster* by Laurence Hutton
https://www.gutenberg.org/files/52730/52730-h/52730-h.htm

Fig 121
"Maria F. Malibran," *Portraits in Plaster* by Laurence Hutton
https://www.gutenberg.org/files/52730/52730-h/52730-h.htm

Fig 122
"Senefelder, Alois, 1771-1834," Laurence Hutton Collection
Source: Curtesy of Princeton University

Fig 123
"Caunt, Ben, 1815-1861," Laurence Hutton Collection
Source: Curtesy of Princeton University

Fig 124

"La Bourdonnais, L. C., 1796?-1840," Laurence Hutton Collection
Source: Curtesy of Princeton University

Fig 125
"Reinhardt, Max, 1873-1943;" Laurence Hutton Collection
Source: Curtesy of Princeton University

Fig 126
"Brunel, Marc Isambard, Sir, 1769-1849," Laurence Hutton Collection
Source: Curtesy of Princeton University

Fig 127
"Richard Brinsley Sheridan," *Portraits in Plaster* by Laurence Hutton
https://www.gutenberg.org/files/52730/52730-h/52730-h.htm

Fig 128
File:Dolly death mask.jpg
Author: Manfred Werner, License: CC Attribution-Share Alike 3.0 Unported
https://commons.wikimedia.org/wiki/File:Dolly_death_mask.jpg

Printed in Great Britain
by Amazon